P9-DNB-554

SHATNER
RULES

SHATNER RULES

Your Guide to Understanding the
Shatnerverse and the World At Large

William Shatner
with Chris Regan

DUTTON

DUTTON
Published by Penguin Group (USA) Inc.
375 Hudson Street, New York, New York 10014, U.S.A.
Penguin Group (Canada), 90 Eglinton Avenue East, Suite 700, Toronto, Ontario M4P 2Y3,
Canada (a division of Pearson Penguin Canada Inc.); Penguin Books Ltd, 80 Strand, London
WC2R 0RL, England; Penguin Ireland, 25 St Stephen's Green, Dublin 2, Ireland (a division
of Penguin Books Ltd); Penguin Group (Australia), 250 Camberwell Road, Camberwell,
Victoria 3124, Australia (a division of Pearson Australia Group Pty Ltd); Penguin Books India
Pvt Ltd, 11 Community Centre, Panchsheel Park, New Delhi–110 017, India; Penguin Group
(NZ), 67 Apollo Drive, Rosedale, Auckland 0632, New Zealand (a division of Pearson New
Zealand Ltd); Penguin Books (South Africa) (Pty) Ltd, 24 Sturdee Avenue, Rosebank,
Johannesburg 2196, South Africa

Penguin Books Ltd, Registered Offices: 80 Strand, London WC2R 0RL, England

Published by Dutton, a member of Penguin Group (USA) Inc.

REGISTERED TRADEMARK—MARCA REGISTRADA

ISBN 978-0-525-95251-0

Printed in the United States of America
Set in Adobe Garamond   Designed by Alissa Amell

I've gotten to the age where I am counting every precious minute, so although none of us knows what is going to happen next, the dice are loaded for me having less time than more. So it seems that I should give a giant shout-out to everything meaningful in my life, 'cause you never know when you are going to get another shout-out. So to my wife, my daughters, my grandchildren, my dogs, my horses, and my friends, I hope I see you all tomorrow. And I'd also like to give a shout-out to Chris Regan, who is a terrific guy, a wonderful writer, and a new friend.

CONTENTS

CONTENTS

CONTENTS

It's Shatner's universe. We just live in it.

—PRESIDENT BARACK OBAMA, AS TOLD TO WILLIAM SHATNER*

[*] RULE: Always Take Shatner's Word for It,

Even If You Suspect He's Lying

SHATNER
RULES

RULE: Start Every Book with an Introduction

, William Shatner, am now eighty years of age, and I've been thinking a lot lately about my late mother's eighty-fourth birthday.

Actually, I'm not really thinking of the *exact* date of her birthday as much as I am thinking about the *observance* of her eighty-fourth birthday. It was observed many times in her eighty-fourth year.

We were in a restaurant—me, my two sisters, our respective spouses, and Mother Shatner, who was beaming from ear to ear. Why was she a-beam? Well, a retinue of handsome waiters surrounded her, bellow-singing "Happy Birthday" as only struggling young actors can. A small slice of cake sat in front of her, its sole candle missing its eighty-three siblings, waiting to be blown out by the happy old lady.

And while Mother Shatner and the waiters smiled, her children and assorted family members scowled.

Why?

Well, it was not my mother's eighty-fourth birthday.

That event had passed a few months previous. And once again, my family was mortified by my mother following what had become an important "rule" in her life.

The rule was: "When Dining Out, Always Tell the Waiter It's Your Birthday. That Way You Always Get Free Cake."

The rule suddenly appeared in my mother's code of personal conduct rather late in life, and it was exercised often. She didn't care that her family was embarrassed or that she was lying, committing a low-level form of dessert fraud. All she cared about was the possibility of free cake.

And it's only now, as I approach the same age my mother was those many years ago, that I realize what a . . . *great* . . . rule this is.

It comes down to this: Life is hard; get as much free cake as you possibly can. My mother deserved it, I deserve it, and you deserve it. And make a wish when you blow out the candle. (I call dibs on "I Wish I Could Fly," though.)

With *Shatner Rules,* I hope to share some of the principles that have governed my very existence over the years, and how I have applied them in real-life situations. My life has been a unique, strange, and wonderful one, and I hope these rules are suitably unique, strange, and worthy of some measure of wonder.

By the end of this tome, will you learn how to live a Shatner-esque existence? Yes. Will you experience the essence of Shatner in its purest form? Absolutely. Will you *be* Shatner?

Of course not. There can only be one Shatner. I am he, and have been for eighty years.

Besides, as we learned on television many years ago, a "mirror" version of me is often an evil me.

Happy reading. Go get your free cake!

My Best,

Bill*

Studio City, California

2011

In the course of this book, you'll realize that Bill is a slightly different guy from Shatner. Bill's pretty laid back, a regular guy, a lot like you. Sometimes Shatner relaxes into Bill. Even Shatner can't keep up the Shatner all the time.

CHAPTER 1

RULE: Say "Yes"

"**N**o!"

Leonard Nimoy flat-out said "no."

"But what do you mean, Leonard? You're my friend! You *have* to be there. I want you there!" I implored.

"No—absolutely not. Have you seen those things? They're devastating! They're brutal! I cannot and will not attend. And you shouldn't, either."

There would be no changing his mind. Leonard Nimoy would have no part of "The Comedy Central Roast of William Shatner."

Sure, *he* could walk away, but I didn't have a choice. I had to be in it. Actors love to have their name above the title, but my name was *in* the title! How could I turn that down?!

> **RULE: Always Be Yourself. Especially If "Yourself" Has a High Q Rating and Is Pleasing to a Wide Variety of Advertisers. (See Shatner, William)**

It's important for an actor to avoid typecasting. At one time I was in danger of forever being linked to a science fiction program that

Kirk and Spock reminisce about life on the *Enterprise*, among other more important things, on *Raw Nerve* in 2009.

had a fairly brief network run in the 1960s. But fears of typecasting aside, I've had a much easier time embracing this William Shatner character.

After all, William Shatner is a role I was born to play, and this Shatner guy has become more and more popular over the years. Heck, you're even holding a book *written* by him! Obviously, William Shatner has found a place in your life. In some respects he's become inescapable!

It was only a matter of time before he got roasted.

Now, what did I know of roasts? Well, Dean Martin used to host them on TV in the 1970s. They were gentle, slightly ribald affairs in which celebrities in ruffled tuxedoes would be ribbed by such comedic masters as Don Rickles, Phyllis Diller, Foster Brooks, and the like. Dean would sit off to the side, sipping iced tea that was supposed to resemble scotch, and laugh his head off.

My roast would be different. As anyone who's ever watched a Comedy Central Roast can tell you, no fake booze is allowed on stage. The real stuff flows freely, to both loosen the tongues of the roasters and ease the pain of the roastee.

FUN FACTNER: Andy Dick has appeared on two Comedy Central Roasts. He has no recollection of this!

And even though I had been warned away by more people than just Leonard, I said "yes" to these comedy inquisitors who were about to strap me to the laugh rack on national television. Was I afraid? Of course. But I always bolster myself when embarking on a risky career endeavor by simply repeating my old actor's adage: "Only stuntmen get hurt."

Why did I say "yes"? Well, I nearly always say "yes."

"Yes" means opportunity. "Yes" makes the dots in your life appear. And if you're willing and open, you can connect these dots. You don't know where these dots are going to lead, and if you don't invest yourself fully, the dots won't connect. The lines you make with those dots always lead to interesting places. "No" closes doors. "Yes" kicks them wide open.

RULE: No Means "No!" (Has That Been Taken?)

I seriously considered saying "no" to being in *Boston Legal*. I didn't want to be involved in the series grind. "Yes" earned me two Emmys. I once said "yes" to Decca Records when they approached me about doing an album in 1968. *The Transformed Man* earned itself many a "no" from critics, but that album has led to so many wonderful things in my life: working with Ben Folds, releasing the critically acclaimed *Has Been* in 2004, and racking up millions of YouTube hits for my rendition of Cee Lo's "Fuck You" on *Lopez Tonight*. And saying "fuck yes" to performing "Fuck You" got me a very nice fan letter from Cee Lo.

No, please, the pleasure was all mine, Mr. . . . Lo?

If I spent more of my life saying "no," this autobiographical volume would be a slim one, indeed.

But enough of the touchy feely stuff, let's talk about . . .

. . . my scrotum. And my weight. And my hair. And my acting. And my weight. And my hair. Did I mention my acting?

All these things were fair game for my roasters, all of who were aided and abetted by a crack team of joke writers—men I quickly realized were *not* my friends. These writers, a bunch of schlubby guys in flannel shirts, dropped by my office for a pre-production meeting one day, and before long I realized that they were giving me the once-over, observing my every move, listening to everything I said, piling up ammo to use against me.

And trying to figure out ways to get me on a horse.

I was in the hands of madmen! Guys who would do anything for a laugh! The roast started with me riding through the audience on horseback. Riding a horse into a roaring crowd! Have you ever ridden a horse into a five-star hotel, in front of throngs of cheering and jeering people? It's a thrilling experience, especially if you somehow manage to survive it. The horse could have gotten spooked and thrown me at any moment. If anyone should kill at a roast, it should be a comedian, not a frightened horse.

I love horses immensely, but I never thought I would be riding one to my own televised execution.

Either way, the show began, I survived the ride, and I successfully maneuvered the animal to the stage, to thunderous applause. And even though she didn't dump any manure into the audience, plenty was about to be dumped on me at my seat on the dais.

My seat was my old captain's chair from *Star Trek*. And I was about to enter a hostile galaxy.

Who was roasting me? It was quite a cast of characters. I will list them by name, and then list the personal features that were brutally dissected by the roasters over the course of the evening.

- Jason Alexander (bald, fat, has-been)
- Andy Dick (drunk, homosexual)
- Artie Lange (fat, drunk)
- Kevin Pollak (hack)
- Lisa Lampanelli (unattractive, serial miscegenationist)

- Betty White (aged, horny, lacking in natural personal lubrication)
- Patton Oswalt (nerdy, troll-like, possible mental disability)
- Nichelle Nichols (African American, horny)
- George Takei (George Takei)

The barbs flew in all directions. For over three hours. I was trapped in a maelstrom of assaults against my person. Andy Dick was running about, licking people. I kept a brave smile on my face, but inside I was screaming "KAHHHHHN!!!"

After a while all I could hear was "Hair." "Acting." "Weight." "Singing." "Scrotum."

Seriously? Jokes about my scrotum? The closest the general public has ever come to seeing my scrotum was in 1974's *Big Bad Mama,* and even then it was carefully hidden behind a naked Angie Dickinson. Perhaps I should have brought a naked Angie Dickinson with me as a shield.

I was mortified. When I try to think of a similar public flogging, my mind harkens back to the time I said "yes" to being king of the Bacchus Parade at Mardi Gras in 1987. My duties, as king, would be to wear a glorious ermine robe (imitation), board a float (since this was during *T.J. Hooker,* I assumed I'd be expected to ride the hood of the float for the duration of the parade), and toss chocolate doubloons at drunken revelers.

Easy enough. But at the beginning of the parade, I raised my king's goblet in toast to New Orleans mayor Sidney Barthelemy, and . . . my pants fell down. Right there, in front of all of Mardi Gras. The king's scepter and orbs were on display, and my dignity quickly abdicated.

(NOTE: Taking off your bottom at Mardi Gras does not get you as many beads as taking off your top. Don't make my mistake!)

I still get covered in a cold sweat when I think about the jokes hurled at me at "The Comedy Central Roast of William Shatner," as I had to sit there silently and *take it*! So I would like to take this opportunity to present some of the insults, and the rebuttals I never got to make.

WILLIAM SHATNER'S ROAST INSULTS & REBUTTALS

Patton Oswalt held up a paper bag and said, "Settle a bet—act your way out of this."

I would, but I need to go pick up my two Emmys at the trophy polisher.

"Bill, you are one of our greatest actors. And I think I'm quoting you correctly, right?"

If I looked like I was enjoying myself at the roast, then I am indeed one of our greatest actors. Go ahead and quote me!

"Bill, you have let yourself boldly go!"

It's called "packing on stature"!

"What is that on your head?"

My hair is actually writing its own autobiography, *Captain's Locks*. I will reveal no spoilers in advance of publication.

"The name Shatner sounds like the barbaric yop of a Viking's cock as it splits a mighty elm into kindling that you built a roaring bonfire to cook meat over that you fill your belly with after you ass rape an ice giant."

Ironically, before we emigrated to Canada, the family name was "Barbaric Yop of a Viking's Cock as It Splits a Mighty Elm into Kindling That You Built a Roaring Bonfire to Cook Meat over That You Fill Your Belly with after You Ass Rape an Ice Giant." But my father found it too much to print on a business card.

Lisa Lampanelli declared, "I've read your writing; it sucks out loud. Your next project should be a suicide note."

I'll write *Suicide Note* after I write the book *I Slept with Lisa Lampanelli*.

Nichelle "Lieutenant Uhura" Nichols from *Star Trek*, with whom I shared network television's first interracial kiss, this time invited me to kiss her "black ass"!

Sorry, Nichelle. If I'm going to put my lips on something that bitter and black, I would like a teaspoon of sugar and a side of biscotti.

Finally, George Takei declared, "Fuck you and the horse you rode in on!"

Well, I went home with my wife that night. I did, however, see George walking around later with a bridle and a bouquet of roses, so who knows what happened?

George and I have had our ups and downs over the years. And I must say, he frightened me a little that evening. When he bellowed the "horse you rode in on" line, he had a scary glint in his eyes. It was either madness, the result of cataract surgery (in which case, George, I'm sorry I didn't send a get-well card), or evidence that he has finally been replaced by a replicant. A replicant programmed to "Hate Shatner!" The vitriol that spewed out of George's mouth was terrifying; he has overwhelming rage at me. He has, for many years, been at a heightened state of Shatnerphobia.

After three hours—three long, agonizing hours—it was my turn at the microphone. I would get the final say after a long evening of me (and my horse) being drilled unmercifully about my acting, my hair, my weight, my acting, my hair, and my weight. And my scrotum.

I would need a big opening, a huge joke, and one that announced that *William Shatner is here, and he's not going to take it anymore.* So I opened with . . . "How's the hair?"

Whew. The laugh was huge, and the laughs kept coming. I cut all my roasters off at the knees with a variety of lacerating jibes and withering bon mots, eventually building to "Who the hell *are* you people? Do you know who I am? *I'm William Tiberius Shatner!*"

I gave it as good as I got it, and everyone got theirs. Even the horses *they* rode in on!

Soon it was over. As the advertisers exclaimed, "The Shat hit the fans." I wondered if my "yes" should maybe have been a "no," or even a "NOOOO!!!!"

"The Comedy Central Roast of William Shatner" was one of that network's highest rated programs, and it was eventually nominated for an Emmy for Outstanding Variety, Music, or Comedy Special. (We lost to a Tony Bennett concert special. I wonder how many jokes were made about *his* hair?) Most important, the show introduced me to many new young fans.

What I learned most of all from "The Comedy Central Roast of William Shatner" is that people have some very definite ideas and feelings about this William Shatner character. He's larger than life, he's omnipresent, he's a narcissist, his acting and hair and singing talents are questionable at best, he's a shill, he's a comedy, he's a tragedy, his scrotum sags with age, he speaks . . . very . . . strange . . . ly.

How do I handle all that?

> **RULE: If You're Gonna Be William Shatner, You'll Need a Lot of Scrotum.**

CHAPTER 2

RULE: To Be Shatner, You Must Know Shatner

The jokes at the roast were great, but a tad misinformed. If you're going to joke about William Shatner you should at least know some very basic facts about William Shatner.

1. I was born on March 22, 1931. And if you were able to quickly Itranslate that number into the correct Star Date, I would like you to put this book down and go get yourself some sunshine.
2. I was born in Montreal in a neighborhood called Cote Saint-Luc. It's pronounced "Coat Saint Luck." (It's not, but like most French speakers, we love any opportunity to correct your pronunciation with our own splendid and sexy French tones.)
3. My grandfather, Wolf, changed the family name to Shatner from Schattner. "Wolf" was a creation of his, too, because it sounded much cooler than his birth name, Sheldon.
4. I started acting when I was six, and have never gotten a paycheck for anything other than performing.

5. In college, I appeared in many dramas and musicals. My comedy work was limited to my academic record.

6. My first film was a 1951 Canadian film noir titled *The Butler's Night Off.* I've never seen it.

7. I won the Tyrone Guthrie Award at Canada's Stratford Shakespeare Festival in the 1950s. I recently misplaced it up the backside of one of my roasters.

8. In 1954, I played the character of Ranger Bob on the Canadian version of *The Howdy Doody Show.*

9. One of my earliest television roles was playing Billy Budd in a live staging of the classic, opposite Basil Rathbone. Rathbone was forever associated with playing Sherlock Holmes. Can you imagine that? Being forever linked with an iconic character?

10. Throughout the 1950s, I acted in a variety of live television plays. Live TV was the norm back then, and there was no risk of a Janet Jackson Super Bowl halftime show moment.

11. My first big studio movie was 1958's *The Brothers Karamazov,* which also featured Yul Brynner, Claire Bloom, and Lee J. Cobb.

12. I once got into a fistfight on stage during the Broadway run of *The World of Susie Wong* with Australian actor Ron Randell. For fifty years now, he's ignored my challenges for a rematch! Coward! [EDITOR'S NOTE: Mr. Randell died in 2005.]

13. Since then, I've never, ever punched another actor. (Do birthday punches for Candice Bergen count? She seemed to think so!)

14. I starred in two classic *Twilight Zone* episodes, "Nightmare at 20,000 Feet" and "Nick of Time," both written by Richard Matheson. I also acted in *Alfred Hitchcock Presents* and *The Outer Limits*. Before reality programs, TV networks seemed preoccupied with "quality."

15. I turned down the title role in *Dr. Kildare* because I didn't want to get bogged down with a series. Also, I faint at the sight of fake blood.

16. Eventually, I came around to the idea of doing television, and after the network nixed the first *Star Trek* pilot featuring Jeffrey Hunter as Captain Pike, I was hired to star in the second pilot as Captain Kirk. But enough with the obscure trivia, moving on . . .

17. Just kidding. *Star Trek* never really caught on with audiences, ran for three seasons, and was canceled. I wish I had taken notes at the time, because you people sure do have a lot of questions about it.

18. In the 1970s, I really began to get into horses. I could talk about horses all day. I raise Saddlebreds, a uniquely American breed of horse that emerged in Kentucky around two hundred years ago and is used mainly by rich plantation owners. They are known as "five-gaited horses," meaning that in addition to the walk, trot, and canter, they also do the ambling gaits known as the slow gait and the rack. Seeing one of these animals in action is not unlike watching a ballerina at work. I'm

also a champion reiner. What's reining? Well, it's a champion riding competition that involves . . . Oh, sorry. I'm being told you don't have all day. More on this later.

19. For many years, I suffered from tinnitus. Now, it only flares up when I don't want to listen to all those questions about *Star Trek*.

20. In the 1970s, I began doing television commercials. I've done hundreds. And if you would like to reserve this space for your product or service in the paperback version of this book, please call the publisher. We can work out some sort of arrangement.

21. In 1975, I starred in a television series called *Barbary Coast,* in which I played a nineteenth-century government agent and master of disguise. I think it was a great show, but I notice I'm never invited to speak at *Barbary Coast* conventions.

22. I have written nearly thirty books, and my autobiography, *Up Till Now,* was a best-seller in 2008. You don't need to have read that one before reading this one. But you should definitely buy it. And a backup copy. And the audiobook, too. Just because.

23. Ten years after the original series was canceled, in 1979, Kirk and company hit the big screen with *Star Trek: The Motion Picture,* directed by film legend Robert Wise. Its success led to several more hit films, one of which I directed, and many more Star Trek spin-off TV series.

24. In the 1980s, I played the title role in *T.J. Hooker,* a hit series about a by-the-books LA cop who was always quick to use

his nightstick while kicking asses. The final season moved to Chicago, where I was quick to use my overcoat to keep my ass from freezing off.

25. I own a horse ranch in Kentucky where I raise my Saddlebreds. In order to give the place a true plantation feel, I employ many non-paid interns.

26. From 1989 to 1996, I hosted *Rescue 911,* a reality-based program about 911 emergencies, which managed to save 350 lives over the course of its run.

27. A documentary I produced, *How William Shatner Changed the World*, aired on the History Channel and was nominated for an Emmy. A different documentary, *How William Shatner Rocked Your World,* is a pay-per-view thing you can watch in your hotel room.

28. Much has been made of the supposed fortune I earned as spokesman for Priceline.com. And if you are crass enough to bring up this fact in my presence, I will buy and sell you ten times over!

29. Since 2001, I have been married to a lovely woman named Elizabeth. No joke here, folks.

30. After seeing a Priceline commercial, David E. Kelley created the role of Denny Crane for me. *Boston Legal* ran for several seasons and earned me some of the best notices of my career, along with two Emmy awards. It was maybe the best thing to come out of my Priceline work, second only to my massive fortune.

31. Much has been made of my not appearing in J.J. Abrams's reboot of the Star Trek franchise. More should be made out of the fact that Kirk lands on Delta Vega in the *exact* location that older Spock is. Come on! It's a huge planet! As giant as that coincidence!

32. I starred in the sitcom *$#*! My Dad Says,* the first ever show launched from a Twitter feed. A group called the Parents Television Council was outraged over the title. I said to them, "Don't get your [redacted] in a [redacted]!"

CHAPTER 3

RULE: Busy Is Measured in Units of Shatner

A lot of people reading this book (or listening to the audiobook, in which case I would like to deliver a sexy "hello") want to know the rules of being William Shatner, looking at this tome as a map to certain truths of self-Shatnerhood.

Well, if there is one rule you must follow on your scramble up the pyramid of Shatner's hierarchy, it's this: Stay busy.

So busy, in fact, that you won't have time to sit around and read a book about how busy I am. Put the book down now! (Although you will need to read on to know how to navigate being as busy as I am. This is indeed a conundrum! Keep reading? *Fail!* Stop reading? *Fail! What are you going to do?*)

RULE: Don't Let Shatner Get into Your Head! (Even I Follow This One!)

Where was I? Oh yes, sorry—I am an extraordinarily busy man. I don't have time to write this book, much less edit it. That's why things may jump around a bit here in the narrative of *Shatner Rules.* Look at it as "Shatner playing with the space-time continuum" for those of you who need that sci-fi angle.

Here, let's examine a typical day on my calendar.

March 7, 2011. I'm using the Earth calendar now, but some of you outer space buffs will remember that as the next-to-last day of the final voyage of the Space Shuttle *Discovery.* After twenty-seven years, she was being decommissioned.

My day started off normally: breakfast, exercise, going over lines, and politely asking fans to vacate my lawn. But the crew of the *Discovery* started off their day with a message. From me.

I had the honor, the distinct honor, of providing the wake-up call for the astronauts that morning. This is what I said to the heroes as they orbited our planet, as the theme music from *Star Trek* played.

> **Space, the Final Frontier.**
>
> **These have been the voyages of the Space Shuttle *Discovery.***
>
> **Her thirty-year mission? To seek out new science, to build new outposts, to bring nations together on the Final Frontier.**
>
> **To boldly go and do what no spacecraft has done before.**

(Normally, the only person who gets woken up to my voice is my wife, Elizabeth, and then I'm usually saying something far less eloquent, like "Dear God! Hit the snooze button!")

It was truly a moving moment, especially since I've been involved with NASA from the very early days of the space program. And now I was asked to say "goodbye" on the final voyage of the *Discovery*. It was a milestone in my life, and in the life of the American space program.

And I forgot all about it.

I was just *so* busy that day. I had to be reminded that the message I had recorded a few days previous was being played for the crew that morning. It was in all the papers, but who has time to read papers?

My busy days are measured in degrees of Shatners. And March 7, 2011, was certainly "two Shatners," if not "three Shatners." (A four-Shatner day would make your head explode.)

For one thing, on March 7, 2011, I had just returned from the Emerald City Comicon, a huge sci-fi/fantasy/comic convention in Seattle, Washington. It's like most conventions, but since it's in Seattle, everyone's homemade Romulan outfits are constructed from flannel. There, I spoke to thousands of Star Trek fans, asked questions, signed autographs, and tried to avoid the rain. (Did I mention it was in Seattle?)

My Star Trek convention appearances have made me a better all-around performer. I get to improvise in front of the audience. I have to inform and access my memories, but also entertain. It's comedic riff after riff after riff.

It's a juggling act, but I never lose sight of the fact that the people sitting before me have put down money to see me, and that

I've got to give them my *best*! If I slight them in the most minute fashion, I am slighting myself. I have always strove to the furthest of my ability to perform my best in front of an audience.

RULE: On Occasion, Be Sincere

That being said—*Star Trek* was many, many years ago, and no, I don't remember exactly what I was thinking when I hit that switch and was talking into that painted button and that Romulan did the thing. And no, I can't break down the genetic differences between the Romulans, Klingons, and Vulcans. And no, I won't sign "Live Long and Prosper" on your boob.

(That last one has nothing to do with my memory, but more with the fact that I am a happily married man. Although while walking around Pike Place Market during the Seattle visit, a woman working in a dried fruit and nut stall asked me to sign her "nut sack." I *had* to oblige.)

I hope that fans can understand the fact that I don't remember a lot of that stuff. My memoir *Star Trek Memories* was published in 1993, years closer to the events in question. That might be worth a purchase. Buy two, since there's no audiobook.

My fading memory concerning the show is the reason I always print out this standard answer sheet for my Star Trek conventions for whenever I get stumped. It's a cheat sheet and the answers work for many different kinds of questions. Go ahead; ask me any question, your answer will be here:

**WILLIAM SHATNER'S STANDARD STAR TREK
CONVENTION ANSWERS**

"Leonard, definitely. The other four? Not so much."

"Well, that's a question for Gene Coon."

"Probably 'City on the Edge of Forever,' and you should watch it
  yourself to find out more!"

"Nichelle. Twice."

"That would be 'The Corbomite Maneuver,' which I don't have
  to explain since you've all seen it. Next question."

"When I was a teenager. Don't give up hope."

"Third door on the right."

"Blue."

What else was happening on March 7, 2011? In addition to
recovering from the Comicon, I was preparing for the Genies,
which are the Canadian equivalent of the Oscars.

Why did they ask me? Well, the Oscars had tried to go "young"
and "hip" with James Franco and Anne Hathaway a few weeks
previous, and the results were such that the Genies decided to go
"old" and "me." Either way, the Genies were a thrilling night in
which Denis Villeneuve's *Incendies* won Best Picture over Richard
J. Lewis's *Barney's Version*. (In addition to going "old," the Genies
also differ from the Oscars by going "hopelessly obscure.")

That morning of March 7 also included a conference call with
the comedy writers of the Genies over the phone. We needed to

rewrite and tweak some of their jokes for me. They wrote all the material from the angle that the "William Shatner" character is some sort of brash, egomaniacal lout. Where did they get that idea? Seriously. How dare they? *Few are worthy enough to call me an egomaniac!*

March 7 also saw me preparing for a variety of meetings I was to have in Canada to pitch some new television shows I hope to produce there. These would be in addition to my duties on *$#*! My Dad Says, Shatner's Raw Nerve, Aftermath*, and probably a dozen more by the time this book goes to press. (On most days, I also need to allow some space in my schedule to work on perfecting the Shatner Cloning Technology. If you think I'm ubiquitous now . . .)

Oh, and I also had to write this book you are holding. The one that sits in your idle hands, taking up your free time. "Free time?" *Must be nice!*

So who could blame me for forgetting the Space Shuttle launch, and my role in it? *I was busy.*

What else ate up March 7, 2011? My Dobermans eating up their beds. Yes, my beloved Dobermans decided to get all Doberman on their doggy beds and ripped them to shreds. Perhaps they were craving a bit more attention from their busy, busy owner?

So in addition to recovering from a convention, writing jokes for my Genie appearance, sharpening my show pitches, writing this book, and working on my cloning technologies, I had to run out and get new doggy beds.

Why?

Because that night we were having very special company.

Elizabeth and I like to hold salons occasionally at our house. And that evening we were hosting three experts from UCLA's Mindful Awareness Research Center, or MARC, which is a program dedicated to the study and promotion of mindful awareness. This is very heady stuff, explained by very important people, and I didn't want them covered in doggy bed stuffing.

My guests were Marvin G. Belzer, Ph.D., Susan L. Smalley, Ph.D., and Diana Winston, the director of mindfulness education at UCLA. What is mindful awareness? Well, it's part meditation, really, a state of contemplation, and an awareness of one's own body, feelings, consciousness, thoughts, and one's place in time and space. It's about stopping and breathing. It helps you deal with anxiety, gives you a sense of well-being, and helps you find the calm. Mindfulness meditation tunes you in to everything that's going on at that very minute, deep in that universe inside you. And when you explore your inner universe, you connect more fully with the outer universe.

Mindfulness makes you more empathetic; it strengthens portions of your mind that you want to improve; it helps . . . you . . . cope! With days like March 7, 2011.

At the end of my fourteen-hour day, I had the privilege of sitting with these experts, doing a meditation, and hearing all about their studies at the university. And during our meditations, all the anxieties of not knowing the tiniest details of *Star Trek*'s "The Corbomite Maneuver" (season 1, episode 10), of rewriting jokes about Paul Giamatti's performance in *Barney's Version* for the Genies, of pitching shows to Canadian television, of perfecting my clone, of forgetting all about my part in that day's historic Space Shuttle launch, of writing a fifty-thousand-word guide book called *Shatner Rules*, and of my scrambling to find two matching dog beds in the neighborhood in an hour's time, began to melt away.

How do I keep up on a two- to three-Shatner day? I keep mindfully aware that another day is around the corner, another day for me to play a part, another day for me to get things done, another day to make sure the dogs aren't setting their sights on the sofa.

That's how I do it.

Shatner Gets Serious

As for the final mission of the Space Shuttle *Discovery*, I was honored that my voice was chosen to wake up the crew on their last day in space. My voice was with them, and so was my heart. I believe the space program fills many niches in humanity's psyche, but most important, it waves a banner to mankind that reads, "Look beyond yourself; look to the future; look to what we can do as human beings."

Mindfulness is about the desire to reach beyond our ability to grasp. When monkeys did that, they fell to the ground because they couldn't reach that limb. As a result, they had to walk and as a result, we are bipedal (most of us) and here we are. In reaching for the stars, the ingenuity of man, the requisite teamwork of all mankind, is called upon.

Although honestly, I could use a team to help me through some of these busy, busy days. Send a résumé if you're a hard worker.

RULE: Working as Shatner's Assistant Is Its Own Reward. No Payment Should Be Requested as None Will Be Given. Be Mindful of That.

RULES FOR TURNING 80

This year, 2011, marks my eightieth year. Throughout this book, I will offer up special rules that you will need to follow if you plan on becoming an octogenarian—one with grace, wit, and swagger (fake hip permitting).

FIRST RULE FOR TURNING EIGHTY: Just Smile. You're Lucky You Made It.

Elizabeth and I were at the airport recently, getting ready for our trip to Australia, where I was to appear in a one-man show titled *Kirk, Crane and Beyond: William Shatner Live.* Or at least "semi-live," depending on how bad the jet lag was going to hit me.

Australia would be one of my favorite places on Earth, if not for the fact that it's located all the way the hell in Australia. Seriously, it takes about a day to get there, and you usually "lose" a day in the process. And whenever I travel there, some passenger invariably makes some crack to me about warp speed or something, so on the flight I like to keep my nose buried in as many time-consuming activities as possible. Time does not fly when flying to Australia.

I went to the terminal's newspaper/candy/souvenir shop to browse the selection of hour-erasing magazines, crossword puzzles, playing cards, books, and "natural" sleep aids, most of which prefer the advertising power of the word "natural" over "ineffective."

After having stuffed several magazines and Sudoku collections under my arms, I proceeded to the gentleman behind the counter, who rang up my items. I scoured the celebrity magazines, hoping to maybe see a celebrity. Weren't Kardashians something I used to fight?

The clerk calculated the total, and I plopped down a credit card. He looked at the name on the card, looked at me, back at the card, and at me again. I was wearing a wide-brimmed, floppy hat.

"Is this you?" he asked.

"Uh huh," I responded.

"Seriously?"

"Yes, I am always serious about me."

He took a look at the card again, and peered into my visage, and said, "My. How time flies."

I've been told—I don't remember it—that when I turned forty, I stayed in bed for three days. And not three days in bed in a good way. Getting old is not easy, especially when you're someone whose face is accessible to so many at all times. But . . .

I just smiled at this clerk. When you're an actor, as long as they still recognize the face, that's an achievement. Life is good, career is good, love is good. That's all that matters to me.

Time *does* fly, and it's all good as long as your attitude is flying first class.

(I can probably find you a good deal on the first-class ticket, by the way.)

CHAPTER 4

RULE: Go West, Young Man. And Leave the Map at Home.

lizabeth and I recently pulled into our driveway after a weeklong drive from our home in Kentucky, with a stop in her home state of Indiana, and then on to Los Angeles. I shut off the car, and she turned to me and said, "Let's turn around and get lost again."

And I would have too, if not for the stringent deadlines of a certain fifty-thousand-word rule book/memoir. (We are right now at word 6,471. God knows where we'd be if I'd listened to my wife!)

We traveled nearly four thousand miles and had such a joyous time that we never even once turned on the radio. We just sat beside one another and talked, and shared, and experienced. And if we got lonely for our typical American radio, Elizabeth and I took turns saying bombastic things about the president and giving one another birthday shout-outs!

If you learn anything from *Shatner Rules*, it's that my career has been an adventure, full of unexpected stops, starts, twists, and turns, and my undying allegiance to "yes" and the unexpected. This also extends to my time spent traveling and adventuring.

I love traveling, and I love getting lost. I have a GPS in all my cars, but they are usually switched off. (By the way, isn't it time that *I* became a GPS voice? You can download Gary Busey, KITT from *Knight Rider*, and Flavor Flav. There has to be a market for William Shatner giving you directions! Let's talk, GPS manufacturers. And unlike the sexy lady voice on most units, I can actually pronounce "Sepulveda Boulevard" properly.)

> **RULE: No Voyage Is Complete without a Side Trip to Scenic Self-Promotion Falls, Pop. Shatner**

Getting lost in America, one of my favorite hobbies, is something I first did in college. A buddy of mine from McGill University and I set out to see America in 1948. We were armed with only our backpacks, our youthful exuberance, and two cardboard signs.

What did the signs say?

Remember Burma-Shave? If you are younger than me, you probably don't, and you probably don't shave as much as you should either. Seriously, kids, when did beards become popular again? Last time I attended a Star Trek convention, I thought I was addressing a pack of Civil War reenactors. (Then again, it might have been a Civil War convention. I do a lot of conventions.)

Well, Burma-Shave had a unique and wonderful way of advertising its product. They would line the highways of America with a set of sequential signs, each sign having the line of a poem on it. The entire nation was covered with the terrific little stanzas promoting the clean shave of Burma-Shave brushless shaving cream.

A few examples:

Does your husband / Misbehave / Grunt and grumble / Rant and rave / Shoot the brute some / Burma-Shave

Your shaving brush / Has had its day / So why not / Shave the modern way / With / Burma-Shave

A peach / Looks good / With lots of fuzz / But man's no peach / And never wuz / Burma-Shave

Great, funny, memorable advertisements. Had they not folded in 1963, taking their signs with them, I would have loved to have worked with them and endorsed their fine product!

Anyway, my college buddy and I held two pieces of cardboard, like the Burma-Shave signs, which read:

Two McGill Students / Seeing the US.

> **RULE: If You Really Want to Re-create the Burma-Shave Magic, Travel with at Least Four More Friends**

And we would stand a distance from one another along the road, thumbs out, and get picked up by strangers and driven across this strange land.

Unfortunately, about two weeks into our adventure, my buddy bailed on me, leaving me with the sign TWO MCGILL STUDENTS. People weren't sure if I was advertising a sale of two McGill students, or if I wanted two McGill students, or if I was traveling to the city of Two McGill Students in search of employment and/or adventure. Either way, the sign no longer had its Burma-Shave appeal, and I started relying solely on my thumb and youthful good looks.

Now, in this day and age, it is irresponsible for me to suggest that my readers just throw away the map and hop into a car with strangers. Sure, I survived it, but just barely.

I mean, at one point I was picked up by a farmer in a decrepit pickup truck who had a long ponytail. This was 1948. People didn't have long ponytails. But this one did. Part of the adventure—see strange places, meet new people!

He also had fairly progressive views on sexual freedom. Meaning, he felt he had the freedom to explore my sexual bits. His advances were not the kind I was expecting from a resident of America's Corn Belt, but he went straight for my buckle. Needless to say, unlike my voyages with Elizabeth, I suggested that we turn on the radio, play the license plate game—anything to rebuff his amorous advances.

After a while, I thanked him for the ride and got out—as soon as he slowed down to about twenty miles per hour.

(NOTE: If you do a tuck and roll at twenty miles per hour, you will most likely crush your cardboard TWO MCGILL STUDENTS *sign.)*

Perhaps the most memorable leg of my maiden walk across the nation started in Pennsylvania, when an elderly rabbi and his wife picked me up. It was midday on a Wednesday, and the elderly Talmudist told me that he needed to get to Chicago by sundown Friday. I could get a lift from them, but I would be the one driving their car.

Easy, you say? Those of you with your GPS systems and interstate highways.

This was 1948. Dwight D. Eisenhower's Federal Aid Highway Act, which provided a road map for our nation's highways, wasn't signed until 1956. There weren't many highways then, only byways. If I was going to make it to Chicago in forty-eight hours, I was going to need to step on it. Warp speed!

With a sleeping ancient rabbi in the backseat. Who would wake up every time I hit a bump in the road, which were plentiful in the days before the Federal Aid Highway Act of 1956. The old man would pop out of the stupor, fix a rabbinical eye on me, and say, "Go slow, boy, go slow." And then his head would fall to his wife's shoulder and I'd continue driving into the night.

Thanks to my precious elderly cargo, I was going much more slowly than I would have preferred when I hit the city limits of Chicago, and the panic set it.

At around 6 P.M., I was zipping around the streets of a strange city, chauffeuring an increasingly panicked rabbi in the backseat, who was looking at his watch and lamenting the setting sun, which was now vanishing behind the tall buildings.

"The sun is down!" he wailed. "You promised! We have taken you across country and you have broken your promise to a rabbi!"

The William Shatner seated at his computer now would have shrugged off such lamentations, but the William Shatner in this story was a seventeen-year-old Jewish kid from Montreal raised by Conservative parents. This wasn't a narcoleptic octogenarian scolding me; God was scolding me.

And when faced with the word of God, there is no better time for the emergence of The Negotiator.

Yes, this may have been the first time my personage was taken over by the spirit of The Negotiator, but as I clutched the steering wheel, one eye on the road, the other scanning the buildings for the address of this temple, I began to debate the old man on what exactly "sundown" meant.

I mean, were we talking God's sundown? Or man's sundown?

The rabbi was perplexed. "What is the difference?" he asked.

"Well, God's sundown," I vamped, "is determined by God's hills, God's forests, God's horizon line on the sea. I see none of these, and therefore CANNOT determine the exact time of God's sundown."

"Go on," he said, as his wife pulled his watch from his pocket.

"The sun has set behind the buildings. That is true. But who made these buildings?"

"Man," he answered. The teacher was engaging his student, despite our potential violation of the Sabbath.

"Will you allow man to decide when the sun sets?"

"No," he answered, smiling.

"And besides, how much of the sun needs to vanish before it has technically set? Ten percent? Twenty? Seventy-five?"

His wife leaned forward and said, "Okay, sonny—we get it." It was the only thing I remember her saying for the entire journey.

And I squealed to a halt in front of the temple, as the last worshipers were filing in. As the rabbi and his wife exited, he announced his hopes that I would one day enter rabbinical school, and we said our goodbyes.

I was then a seventeen-year-old, alone in the city of Chicago for the first time, with no ride. Needless to say, my thoughts turned away from the theological and I went to explore.

Where did I end up in the Windy City? Who knows? I've always avoided the traditional signposts.

Throw away the map!

When I first went to Broadway in 1956 with *Tamburlaine the Great*, starring Anthony Quayle and directed by my mentor, Tyrone Guthrie, I made a beeline for Forty-second and Broadway. It wasn't what I thought it would be. I did not find my dreams there. My dreams would come true a few blocks away in Schubert Alley, a few blocks north at the Winter Garden Theater, a few blocks over at the Broadhurst, down at the Booth on Forty-fifth.

When I first made the trip to Hollywood in 1958, I decided to take a car. (My first wife wouldn't have appreciated the Burma-Shave thumb method.) And we drove straight to Hollywood and Vine. It was another spot on the map that led to disappointment.

It was seedy, grimy. Was this where my Hollywood dreams were to come true?

No, there were no studios at Hollywood and Vine, and I didn't see any dancing girls at Forty-second and Broadway. We are led to believe these are such glamorous crossroads, and they are anything but. If you have to use a map, move away from the pinpoints and allow yourself a little more compass room, provided you haven't thrown away your compass. The journey must be taken in individual moments. Enjoy the ride for the ride.

What am I trying to say? Perhaps I should grab a marker and some pieces of cardboard.

As you travel / Over hill and dale / Go get lost / But watch out for the ponytail!

QUIZ

This simple quiz will test your understanding of the *Shatner Rules* so far. Please use pencil in case you need to erase.

1. Would you like to take a quiz?

Yes_____

No_____

ANSWER KEY

What part of "Say 'yes'" don't you understand? If you answered "yes," please continue to the next page. If you answered "no," then please go back to page 1, and start again. But enjoy again my roast barbs. I'm particularly proud of the Lisa Lampanelli one!

CHAPTER 5

RULE: Stay Hydrated

O kay, they don't all have to be funny. This one is important. Especially for an actor.

I was on Broadway in the play *A Shot in the Dark* in 1961, along with Julie Harris and Walter Matthau. It was a French farce that was later retooled as an Inspector Clouseau film for Peter Sellers. And by "retooled," I mean "un-Shatnered."

The play was directed by the legendary director Harold Clurman, who became something of a legendary pain in the butt to me. He didn't like my performance in the show, and always told me I was "playing the charm" rather than acting. What's worse—he wouldn't tell me what "playing the charm" actually meant.

These kind of tensions make for rocky performances, and early in the run of the show, during previews, I "dried" on stage. What does that mean? It means, um . . . what does it mean . . . now . . . it, um . . . wait for it . . . it means, um . . .

RULE: Don't Forget Your Lines!

Again—not all these rules are jokes! Forgetting your lines is a terrifying thing for an actor. I was onstage, completely lost, and the only sound I could hear was the beating of my heart. And the sound of Harold Clurman in the audience, gasping in exasperation with me, rising up from his seat in the first row, and stomping all the way up the aisle in anger. At least his tantrum distracted the audience from the actor on stage who had drawn a lengthy and devastating blank.

I might have been playing the charm, but I seemed unable to *turn on* the charm, especially when it came to Harold Clurman. This was especially hard on me because I had long admired his work with New York's legendary Group Theater in the 1930s. He directed the first production of Clifford Odets's *Golden Boy*, whose main character, Joe Bonaparte, was a character I strongly identified with as a teen. He's a violinist who is seduced by the big-money world of boxing. As a kid who loved acting but who hid it from his football pals, I could clearly identify with the conflict of straddling both worlds. Now, my experience with Clurman had me straddling the two worlds of employment/unemployment.

(NOTE: While I tried my best to keep my thespianic desires secret from my football chums, I was exposed as an actor by a high school history teacher who knew I had the bug and who tasked me with reciting Marc Anthony's act 3, scene 1 speech from Shakespeare's Julius Caesar *to the entire class.*

Everyone was staring at me with great suspicion as I walked to the front of the classroom and tore into the speech, but by the time I bellowed, "Cry havoc and let slip the dogs of war!" all my teammates were standing up and crying havoc themselves. Seriously, there was almost a mini riot.)

I didn't forget my lines again during the rest of the run of *A Shot in the Dark,* but an evening or two after I metaphorically "dried," I literally "dried" on stage during previews. My throat began to tickle, and soon I had a full-fledged coughing fit on stage. Fortunately, my hacking was drowned out by the familiar sound of Harold Clurman having a coronary and throwing another stompfest in the audience.

I vowed this was never going to happen to me again, so the evening before our opening night, I took the prop guy aside, pointed to a desk my character sat at during the show, and told him, "Make sure there is a glass of water in that desk every night." If I felt a coughing fit coming on, I could always stroll over to the desk, open a drawer, and take a sip. A *charming* sip, mind you, so as not to disappoint my director.

The play was a hit, and ran for nearly four hundred performances at the Booth Theatre on West Forty-fifth Street in New York. And I think it was during performance 399 that the tickle hit me in the throat again.

I was doing a scene with my beloved costar Julie Harris (who tried her best to get Clurman to like me) when the tickle hit, and remembering my instructions to the prop guy, I sauntered on over to the desk for my throat-saving swig. I kept the coughs at bay as

Julie delivered her line, opened the drawer of my desk, and produced the glass of water.

The glass of water that had been placed in the desk nearly a year before.

RULE: Always Remember to Schedule a Follow-Up Meeting with the Prop Guy

About half the water had evaporated, leaving a thick, white crust in its wake. At least it looked like a white crust, having been obscured by a year's worth of theater dust. The water that was left was greenish, covered in a film, and—believe it or not—bubbling slightly. I felt like one of the witches in *Macbeth* with this toxic, green, bubbling brew in my hand.

My stomach muscles tightened, to keep the coughs—and my lunch—down. Julie had finished her line and turned to me. If I opened my mouth then, I would have gotten two, three words out before everything fell apart in a hacking cough. I could almost hear Clurman warming up for his tirade.

I put the glass to my lips and I swallowed every last drop of sludge. I placed the glass down, and slapped my hands on the desk—once, twice, three times. Julie saw what I had done and looked at me with horror. I could feel the thick water clinging to the sides of my throat as the sludge made its way down, contaminating my insides in its wake.

I swallowed hard, opened my mouth, and . . . no tickle. Gone. The toxic brew had done its job. I was able to proceed. With aplomb. With dignity. With bearing. And . . . with . . . charm!

(NOTE: What emerged from my insides shortly after the curtain was anything but charming.)

CHAPTER 6

RULE: It's Good to Bury the Hatchet——So Your Former Costars Won't Find It and Use It on You

Never go to bed angry. Unresolved anger can destroy even the strongest of relationships. And for God's sake—unresolved anger has no business being at anyone's wedding! And I've had four weddings. I'm an expert.

Which brings me to the story of the marriage of my old *Star Trek* colleague George Takei, who played Lieutenant Hikaru Sulu.

There's been a great deal of enmity between George and me. He's been saying mean things about me for nearly forty years now. That's nearly Star Trek (Two) Generations! Criticizing me publicly, in every venue imaginable! He says that I have a "big, shiny, ego!" Well, actors have big egos. If mine is shiny, it's because I tend to it very carefully and lovingly.

Perhaps George's needs a good polish.

To be fair, George is not the only veteran of the USS *Enterprise* who has hard feelings. Walter Koenig has been vocal about his disdain for me, James Doohan was not a fan, and Nichelle Nichols told me—while I was interviewing her for my book *Star Trek Memories*—that she detested me. Set phasers to Awkward!

All this animosity! I guess I could blame myself, but the things I really blame . . . are the Star Trek conventions.

There, I said it.

Now, the conventions have been good to me over the years, I enjoy going to them. I smile politely when a fellow comes up to me and asks for my autograph in the native Klingon tongue.

(NOTE: When someone speaks to you in Klingon, say "nuqjatlh?" *It's Klingon for* "huh?" *That usually wraps up the conversation pretty fast.)*

But in the early days, I didn't attend them. Wouldn't go near them. *Star Trek* was a job I did for three years, it ended, I moved on. I fear my fellow cast members did not, and were hopelessly stuck in Stardate 2999.9 and operating on the Prime Directive of "Hate Bill."

The supporting cast, some of whom I wouldn't see for days or even weeks at a time during our initial filming schedule due to the size of their roles, would later attend the conventions and be greeted with cheers. Fans would tell them that their characters should have been given more to do! Had their own series!

Now, had they been the *stars* of *Star Trek,* they *would* have been there every day on set. Like I was. And Leonard. And DeForest Kelley. And maybe they would have gotten their own shows.

And I'm all for spin-offs, but they never happened.

FAILED *STAR TREK* SPIN-OFFS

Montgomery's Ward: Montgomery "Scotty" Scott retires to run a
haggis shop and is forced to raise an irascible teenager named
Lulu. He threatens all her boyfriends with "opening up a big can
of fully activated phaser bank!"

Uhura-Who?: Uhura suffers amnesia, sits around, and monitors the
frequency of a nearby ATM machine.

Warp & Windy: Mr. Sulu tries his hand as a weatherman at a small-
town television station. His catchphrase? "There will be rain
this weekend. Engage Slickers!"

And I believe the adoration of these supporting actors at conventions led to a mutiny against their beloved captain. There were
allegations that I stole lines from cast members, close-ups, someone's lunch out of the fridge. No comment on that last one.

> RULE: If You Don't Write Your Name on Your Lunch, I
> Write "William Shatner" on It

And I have apologized time and time again for whatever it was I
supposedly did. In the press, on the television, in the pages of my
books, and in person.

But there is one thing I will not apologize for. There is a hierarchy in show business, which I did not invent. The stars get the

preferential treatment. That's how it is. The people who are paid less, based on billing, get less attention. The main character in *Star Trek* was James T. Kirk. He narrated the show. He was . . . *captain* of the ship upon which the stars were trekked! And traditionally, the stars of shows and films get more lines, more close-ups, and a slightly larger dressing room.

My costars, however, seem to have crossed into a mirror universe due to a transporter malfunction, and they have flipped this hierarchy. Once, while posing for a publicity photo for one of the *Star Trek* movies, the photographer dared put me/Kirk front and center. And I very clearly heard Jimmy Doohan exclaim, "Why is he always up front? I'm tired of being in the back!"

Keep in mind, Jimmy didn't have a Scottish accent in real life, so remarks like that sounded much less charming.

I have also been accused of "counting" lines. I won't dignify this with an explanation, but if you count the lines of any given *Star Trek* script (not that I have), you can clearly see that Kirk has more lines than Scotty. Or so I have been told. Because Kirk is the main character. Not ego. Fact.

That's what I've been up against. And no one has held it against me more than George Takei.

George buys into the stolen close-ups/lines stuff, and he also claims I kept his character from getting his own Federation starship in the movies. I remember a conversation we had quite clearly, as it was right before we shot one of the films.

GEORGE: Bill, they're giving me my own starship.

WS: Why would you want that? All the action's on the *Enterprise.*

GEORGE: But . . . it will be *my* starship.

My statement that "all the action's on the *Enterprise*" later somehow constituted my ruining the commission chances of George/Sulu. George Takei obviously believes I'm a man of tremendous, limitless power. No wonder I have such a big, shiny ego!

Anyway, George announced he was going to marry his long-time partner, Brad Altman, in 2008. I was very happy for him; it's always wonderful when someone finds true love. And then promptly afterward, George announced I was not invited to the wedding.

Should that announcement have been his first priority? Should that have even been an announcement?

Shouldn't he have been busy picking out a wedding DJ? Buying the rings? Constructing a William Shatner piñata for the reception?

Well, needless to say, the only invitation I got from George was an invitation to a knock-down, drag-out fight in the tabloids. He later flip-flopped and said that I *had* been invited, but that I failed to RSVP.

What can you do when confronted with such bizarre behavior? I just shrugged and said, "Oh my!" (There, George, I stole *that* from you. Happy?)

> **RULE:** Always Invite Shatner to Your Wedding. He'll Be Able to Negotiate "Love, Honor, and Obey" Down to "Like, Generally Respect, and Sure Thing, Whatevs!"

George managed to generate a great deal of publicity for his marriage, and the wedding party looked like the speaker's schedule at a Star Trek convention. Walter Koenig, Ensign Pavel Chekov, was George's best man, while Lieutenant Uhura, Nichelle Nichols, was maid of honor. I can only assume that Yarnek, the rock creature, performed the ceremony and the Green Slave Girl from Orion was the ring bearer.

These three actors have been engaged in a long-running plural marriage, tied together in blessed bonds of acrimony. Toward me. The wedding party featured a triumvirate of people who hate me. All sharing George's special day.

FUN FACTNER: If the Sulu from the animated Star Trek cartoon had gotten married, he would never have invited Chekov to his wedding because Chekov wasn't even in the cartoon! (Seriously, George! Walter and not me?! Come on!)

I had questions for these three. And like most people who have questions, I have a national television show on which to ask them.

I asked George to be a guest on my program *Raw Nerve*, which is about to return for its third season on the Biography Channel. In fact, all the episodes are available on iTunes for $1.99 each. Why don't we take a break in our narrative so that you, dear reader, can go and catch up on this edgy and offbeat celebrity interview series? Go ahead. I'll wait here.

FUN FACTNER: *The Baltimore Sun* said that *Raw Nerve* was "the most intriguing conversation you will find on the tube." That's a not a fact really . . . just my shiny ego talking again. But really, you should check out *Raw Nerve*.

George would have been terrific on *Raw Nerve*, but he did not seem to think so. He thought he was going to be sandbagged or something, and refused to appear on my show and talk it out. Since he is a regular on *The Howard Stern Show*, I even sweetened the deal by saying we could conduct the interview in the Stern studio—presumably while surrounded by lesbians and little people in bondage gear. Nothing.

So I did the next best thing and asked Walter onto the show. And I promised we would both have the same exact number of close-ups throughout the interview. He agreed, and we sat down.

RULE: Keep Your Friends Close, and Your Enemies across from You on Your Talk Show

I got right to the subject of the wedding. I asked him, "Do you know George that well?"

"No," he replied.

No?

Ideally your best man is your most trusted companion in the whole world. He is the man who holds the rings, ushers the guests, and makes the toast. The best man should be the best friend!

I continued, incredulous. "You were his best man. How did that work?"

He looked at me, and paused. I then asked one of the toughest questions I have ever asked on *Raw Nerve*.

"Walter . . . what the fuck?"

FUN FACTNER: "Walter . . . what the fuck?" is William Shatner's "Mr. Gorbachev, tear down this wall!"

He said, "Yeah, you're right. 'What the fuck?' I think he used me."

Walter was used. George added "special guests" to his wedding party, not "friends." It was a branding opportunity. And, like usual, I got branded CLOSE-UP STEALER right in the middle of my forehead.

RULE: Love Means Always Having to Say You're Sorry . . . to Your *Star Trek* Cast Mates

Let me make it clear: George, Walter, Nichelle, Bruce Mars (who played Kirk's nemesis Finnegan in the classic episode "Shore Leave"), I don't know what I did. I apologize. (And honestly, I don't know if Bruce Mars had any hard feelings. Just covering my bases.)

The fact of the matter is, we're all going to die soon. Honestly. We're all really old people. Don't you want to go out with having less enmity than before? This feud is the damnedest thing I've ever seen.

I still have hope that we can all be friends, and put everything behind us. I would have loved to have gone to your wedding, George. I had an inscribed copy of my memoir *Up Till Now* ready to give you as a gift. (I took the liberty of picking that gift out myself. For some reason it wasn't on your registry.)

Don't despair, though; you can still buy a signed copy at WilliamShatner.com. You appear on pages 121 and 148 of the hardcover. I say nice things.

CHAPTER 7

RULE: Get the Damn Line Right!

"**B**eam me up, Scotty."

It is one of the most famous catchphrases in popular culture. Perhaps you've seen it on a bumper sticker, along with the humorous addendum, ". . . There's no intelligent life down here." That's a rather haughty commentary on the intelligence of others from someone who likes to litter his/her car with bumper stickers.

(NOTE: This is not to be confused with a more "Rapture-ready" bumper sticker I've seen, which reads "Beam me up, Lord!" Ironically, if the Rapture does occur, Jews like myself aren't supposed to be "beamed up" by God. I can't believe there is such a flaw in the reasoning of people who are awaiting the Rapture! Either way, like it or not God, I'm getting into Heaven. I can negotiate anything!)

The famed line has appeared on mugs, fridge magnets, and T-shirts, and corrupt Ohio congressman James Traficant would end his House of Representatives floor speeches with the phrase.

(Unfortunately, no one beamed him up before he was sent away to federal prison for a few years.)

"Beam me up, Scotty" has been used as a lyric in dozens of popular songs by such artists as Kid Rock, Jimmy Buffett, Erykah Badu, Nicki Minaj, and R. Kelly. It's been used in too many television shows to count: *Family Guy, Stargate SG-1, Bones, Heroes, Gilmore Girls, Friends, Futurama,* and *Robot Chicken.* In an episode of *South Park,* the Latin version of the phrase was used: *"Me transmitte sursum Caledonii."* And honestly, if the Catholic Church would update their masses with Latin phrases such as these, they might see a spike in attendance.

James Doohan used *Beam Me Up, Scotty* as the title of his autobiography. I imagine the working title of that book was *Things I Hate about Shatner, Vol. 1.*

Yes, people around the world all know the phrase "Beam me up, Scotty." What many people *don't* know is that it was never used in the television show *Star Trek.*

Like "Play it again, Sam," "Elementary, my dear Watson," and "Luke, I am your father" (whatever *that* means), "Beam me up, Scotty" is one of pop culture's most famous misquotations. We said, "Scotty, beam us up," we said, "Scotty, beam me up," we said, "Beam them out of there, Mr. Scott," we said, "Scotty, beam up Kirk, unless you are concerned that the process of beaming will give him a close-up." (Okay, that one is a lie, but it would make a funny T-shirt.)

RULE: William Shatner Likes It When You Send Him T-Shirts You've Made (HINT)

None of this has stopped people from using the phrase "Beam me up, Scotty." And it has not stopped people from shouting it at me over the last forty-odd years.

Ever since the early 1970s, when the show grew exponentially in popularity through syndication, part of the price of being me is that many folks think I like to have "Beam me up, Scotty" yelled, screamed, and shouted at me.

You know, I've been acting since 1937—I have done other work! Feel free to clip out this handy guide and keep it in your wallet for the next time you see me in person.

SUGGESTED THINGS TO SCREAM AT SHATNER BASED ON HIS WORK (OUTSIDE OF THE *STAR TREK* CANON)

"Put on a fake mustache, Agent Cable!"

I played nineteenth-century government agent Jeff Cable in the short-lived 1975 ABC series *Barbary Coast*. The character wore many disguises. It makes sense!

"Let's keep America free, brave, and white!"

This is a super-obscure nod to a line I delivered as the racist hatemonger in Roger Corman's *The Intruder*. Please make sure not to shout this one at me in a public place.

"Where's your naked Angie Dickinson?"

Another nod to the Roger Corman universe, this time to the film *Big Bad Mama*. It's okay to shout this one in a public place, but please make sure I am not with Mrs. Shatner or my grandkids.

"Hey, Dad? Say some bleep!"

Okay, this one is a little awkward. And frankly, I'm still smarting that the show got canceled.

Despite the facts at hand, people have just stuck with "Beam me up, Scotty," and eventually I got used to having it shouted at me.

Mockery is a tricky thing with me. Laughing *with*? Fine. Laughing *at*? Trouble. But the problem about laughing *with* is that sometimes you mistakenly join in the derision.

I certainly understand that shouting "Beam me up, Scotty" to a total stranger is a way to connect . . . with a total stranger. I'm a total stranger who's been barging into everyone's living rooms for the past half century, so I guess some folks feel a kind of connection when they see me.

I brought my car in to be repaired a few weeks back, and the mechanic said, "Must be weird that people come up to you assuming they know you." He thought about it for a second and added, "You know, we *do* know you, because you're in our lives daily."

> **RULE: Even If You're a Mechanic Who Wisely Hits upon a Core Issue Concerning My Existence and Place in the World While Working on My Car, I'm Still Going to Haggle with You about These So-Called Labor Charges**

I was always proud of my work on that low-budget, always-about-to-be-canceled science fiction show. I was proud of the fact that I was able to breathe some human life into a series that sometimes had little physical connection to the real world, all the while trying to remember nonsense words while talking into a cardboard prop. But at some point, as a defense mechanism, I just joined in on the big joke.

In fact, I got *in* on the joke to protect myself *from* the joke.

A few years back I appeared on a British talk show and was having a nice time, when suddenly the host said, "Take a look at this." He then proceeded to show a clip from *T.J. Hooker,* an out-of-context clip. Taking something out of context is the stock and trade of the prankster, and my performance in this clip seemed a little . . . blustery.

The audience laughed while the clip ran, not knowing anything about the reasons for Hooker's bluster, or the choices I made as an actor while trying to convey the emotions. I could see what this host was trying to do. He was laughing *at.*

When the lights came up, he was readying his quip, and I jumped in with, "My God, that was awful." He had nowhere to go, the crowd laughed along with me, and we moved on.

Did I think my performance was awful? No—the lines were a little overheated; the emotions were the kind that you found throughout television drama in the 1980s. Hooker was written as a walking raw nerve with a badge. He was played so accordingly.

If I have been involved in some subpar projects over the years, I can assure you the preparation and discipline I brought to the roles was always way above par.

Discipline. In my many years of performing, I have never once taken a sick day. Not one. I was deathly ill with the flu during the filming of a *Star Trek* episode, and rather than call in sick, I had the producers put a cot down next to the set. In between takes, I would collapse, toss and turn in a cold sweat, and be mopped up in time for the next take. I barely had the strength to steal a close-up! I would not call in sick!

> **RULE: If Shatner Works in Your Office during Flu Season, *Everyone's* Getting the Flu**

Here's what I think: I'm a good actor. I know what to do, I can make you laugh, I can make you cry, and I can always find the good moments. I can say the words so that they have some meaning to them. There are thousands of actors out there in Hollywood, and producers throughout the years have scribbled WILLIAM SHATNER onto some of the checks that they've cut, for varying sizes. They could have written someone else's name. They didn't.

For close to seventy-five years now, since I was a kid, I have been acting. I have never made money for anything other than performing. That is not a joke.

MOCK NEWSPAPER REVIEW FROM 1930s

> Also in the Little Players' production of *Red Riding Hood* was young Billy Shatner as a tree. A solid performance, although this critic sometimes found he was playing the charm. Also, why would a tree shout "KAHN!" in the middle of the second act?

But for many, it seemed *Star Trek* was a joke. And I got in on it.

All those people yelling "Beam me up, Scotty" must have thought that the show, and Kirk, were subjects worthy of mockery. And to protect myself, I joined them. As with that British talk show host, I have tried to beat the mockers to the punch. I soon started laughing and giving a thumbs-up whenever someone shouted the line to me. To many, *Star Trek* is tacky, a campy joke, and so was my performance. Best thing to do is laugh the loudest, right?

And I kept laughing until I made *The Captains.*

The Captains is a feature-length documentary I produced in which I traveled around the world and interviewed everyone who has played a captain within the *Star Trek* canon. I sat down with Scott Bakula (*Star Trek: Enterprise*), Kate Mulgrew (*Star Trek: Voyager*), Avery Brooks (*Star Trek: Deep Space Nine*), and Patrick Stewart (*Star Trek: The Next Generation*). Even Chris Pine, the latest incarnation of Kirk, sat down for a one-on-one.

During the filming, I flew to London to meet Patrick Stewart. For the flight I was seated in the quiet of the wonderful jet that my sponsors at Bombardier generously provided for me . . .

RULE: Never Forget a Plug—Especially One That Keeps You out of the Security Line at the Airport

. . . and in the luxurious quiet of the cabin (thank you again, Bombardier) I was studying my notes on this portrayer of Jean-Luc Picard.

Stewart and I had worked together before, on the film *Star Trek: Generations,* but I didn't know him all that well. We had a scene together in that film where he and I were riding horses, and I gave him the handy tip of wearing panty hose under his clothes to prevent chafing in the saddle.

(NOTE: Tell British actors that they should wear panty hose under their pants while riding horses to prevent chafing. They often fall for it.)

Either way, I had a great epiphany with Stewart and with my

place in the world as a guy forever associated with Captain Kirk. It was a total paradigm shift for me!

I had gotten in on the joke, but for Patrick Stewart there is no joke to be had with *Star Trek*.

Patrick is a marvelous Shakespearean actor. He spent his life doing the classics, and he said "yes" to being in *Star Trek: The Next Generation*. And I soon realized that he approached his performance with the same respect and reverence that he reserved for the Bard.

As I considered this wonderful actor taking *Star Trek* so seriously, I thought, *I haven't done that in a long time*. There was a fullness of his pride in playing that role and doing it well. I wanted that pride back.

And I took it back.

Somewhere along the way I got lost and caught up in the derisive laughs of the haters.

> **RULE: Every So Often, Beam Up One of Your Grandkids to Help You Brush Up on the Modern Slang**

My encounter with Stewart was a revelation for me. I'm proud of my work as Captain Kirk, and it helped carry the viewer into a fantastic faraway world often populated by creatures in rubber suits. No more laughing *at* for me. Sorry folks.

My three years of work on that show, and in the subsequent movies, is much more than the occasional "Beam me up, Scotty" hurled out of a car window. I have once more engaged my shields, and I carry my fictional rank of fictional captain with a great deal of REAL pride.

So go ahead and yell, "Beam me up, Scotty." I have a thing I yell back nowadays, hopefully you'll find it amusing, and it goes . . .

"Fuck you!"

Set phasers on "Oh, Snap!"

CHAPTER 8

RULE: Always Have a Spare Set of Underwear on Hand

Ａnd keep your spare underwear in an undisclosed location. Does this sound silly? Well, let me tell you something: It won't sound silly when you're negotiating with the kidnappers.

Did that wipe the smile off your face? I thought it would! Or did it at least replace your smile with a quizzical stare? Even better!

I was in Denver in the late 1970s, at one of that city's finer hotels. There was a Star Trek convention being held nearby, and I decided to stay in the city for a few days after the event to see the sights. This was back in that dark age when people paid full price for airfare. I was traveling on someone else's nickel, and I thought I would turn it into a mini vacation. So I packed a full bag.

I packed an outfit for my Q&A at the convention, a more formal look for the evenings, and a sportier ensemble for enjoying the many outdoor activities promised by the Mile High City. And since this was the 1970s, there was probably enough polyester in the collection to create a static electricity shock powerful enough to melt a glacier.

The afternoon had included my convention appearance and an autograph session that had to be cut short for a local news interview. Afterward, I got back to my hotel, showered, and then went to my dresser to get ready for dinner. I opened the top drawer, and realized I had been the victim of theft!

My undergarments—every last pair—had been stolen. Someone had snuck in, ignored my camera, some jewelry, and a bit of cash, and decided instead to heist my versatile mix of jockeys and boxers.

Throughout my career, I have received many an honorary title, and I was deputized once or twice. But I had no idea how to access my honorary crime-fighting skills in this situation. I checked all around the room to make sure the culprit wasn't hiding anywhere (and to reassure myself that I hadn't misplaced the garments), and called down to the front desk.

"Hello, how may I help you?"

"I'd like to report a crime," I said to the desk clerk, and gave her my room number.

"I'm sorry to hear that, Mr. Shatner. What was stolen?"

(NOTE: If your name is William Shatner, and you are the victim of an underwear thief, it'll probably make the papers.)

I thought better of it. "Never mind," I said, "I found my . . . stolen things."

The media culture was not the same in the 1970s as it is now.

Today, theft of my unmentionables would be blogged, tweeted, and Facebooked up the wazoo. But even then, in a smallish city, an enterprising reporter could have been listening to a scanner and gotten a scoop about my crime.

Imagine the headlines!

SHATNER SHORTS SWIPED

"ENTERPRISING" THIEVES HEIST HANES

WILL'S WHITEYS: WHERE NO THIEF HAS GONE BEFORE!

I figured I would have to solve this crime myself. Or at least run down to the local Sears and just—

The phone rang. I picked it up. Whoever was calling me was in a crowded place.

"Hello?"

"Mr. Shatner, I have your underwear," said the woman on the other line.

"I see."

"All of it!" she threatened.

"Of course. I'd like it back please."

"Sure, but first you have to do something for me . . ."

"Call me back in three minutes, on this line. I'm calling the shots now!" I hung up the phone.

RULE: If They Do It in the Movies, You Should Do It in Real Life

She had to understand that she was playing with the big boys now. I sat on the bed until she called back.

"Okay, what is it? What do you want?" I said in my best authoritarian voice.

"I'll give you back your underwear, but you have to give me your autograph."

Time to play hardball.

"I spent forty-five minutes giving out autographs today at the convention. Where were you?"

"On line," she snapped. "But then you took off before I got to your table."

Oh dear. Remember all that stuff I wrote about my commitment and dedication to my fans? Well, I've always felt that was important, that's always been my credo, even way back in the early days of the conventions. My interview with the local news station was a contractual obligation, but it's quite possible that this poor woman, this mastermind behind the underwear job, had waited for nearly an hour, only to see me pack up and shuffle off.

She wanted my attention. And rather than grab me by the nuts, she grabbed the things that contain the nuts. I felt guilty, and I at least owed her an autograph. I relented.

"Okay," she said excitedly. "I'll be up to your room in two minutes."

"No way in hell!" I yelled, forgetting the fan loyalty credo, and headed down to the lobby once we agreed on a drop location.

I went down to the lobby and scanned the room. Many folks in town for the convention were staying at the hotel, judging from the number of homemade Federation uniforms worn by the mingling masses. Would my underwear-napper be dressed as Uhura? Would it be a Nurse Chapel, giving my loot the once-over with a cardboard tricorder? Perhaps I should be looking for a lady costumed as the Vulcan matriarch T'Pau, my shorts in her death grip?

Nope. It was a young, seemingly normal woman in her late twenties, seated in an overstuffed chair, gripping a wrinkled brown bag in her lap. Next to her was a largish portfolio of some sort. She nodded to me, keeping it cool.

"Okay, I'll sign whatever," I told her. "Gimme my stuff."

"Not until you sign," she threatened. "What if you just take it and run?"

"I'm not going to sprint across a crowded hotel lobby with a paper bag full of my underwear. Some of us have dignity."

She nodded, handed me the bag, and undid the strings on her leather portfolio. The case opened, revealing a variety of 8×10s of yours truly, from *Star Trek*, *The Twilight Zone*, a few movies, some candids. This was a *fan*.

She pulled the cap off a marker, handed it to me, and began sorting her photos in the order she wanted them signed.

"All of these?" I exclaimed.

"You promised!"

"I promised *an* autograph. Not a dozen. I'll get writer's cramp. I'll be left to pull on my underwear with only one good hand. Pick your favorite and I'll sign it."

She pouted, and sorted through the photos. "Just one? That's all?"

"Yes, one signature," I explained.

She sat back in the chair, smiled, and then bounded up. She pulled down the front of her shirt, revealing her left breast contained in its bra cup, and said, "Autograph my boob."

Dignity. It's always been important to me, and my code of dignity has guided my life. And it then guided me to run across a hotel lobby, holding a bag of my underwear under my arm.

CHAPTER 9

RULE: Eat What You Kill! (Provided It Doesn't Kill You First!)

It was November 1969. Thanksgiving was just around the corner, and I was on all fours, in a dense tunnel of underbrush on California's San Clemente Island. My bow and arrow were slung over my back, and there was barely any room to move. I was hunting.

What was I looking for? What was my prey? A wounded wild boar—one that might come charging at me at any moment, with my arrow sticking out of its bristly hide.

Star Trek's five-year mission had recently been cut short at three years, and in that very moment I wasn't concerned with forever being known as Captain Kirk. In that tunnel, I was now concerned with forever being associated with the newspaper headline ACTOR KILLED BY PIG.

There was only one way out of this tunnel for the massive, tusked, wounded beast, and it was through me.

Now, I have stared down formidable beasts before in the course of my career. Remember Lee Van Cleef? He was a sinister layer of marinara in many a spaghetti Western. In 1963, I was acting in an episode of the anthology program *The Dick Powell Theatre*, in which I played a Swedish (of course) rancher fighting off a hostile land grab by his bigoted neighbors. I played the part with a thick Swedish accent, and in some scenes I wore a too-small bowler hat with a feather.

RULE: Take Some Stuff off Your Résumé

Never mind that rule. The entire episode is on YouTube. You can watch nearly everything I've ever done on YouTube, good and bad, highlights and lowlights. Nearly every week, things I've done in my career that I've long forgotten about come charging back at me, courtesy of YouTube, like a wounded pig in a tunnel.

Which is why I started talking about Lee Van Cleef, right?

Lee was well over six feet tall, a huge man, powerful. And like a wild boar, he had a cold, calculating look. Even when the cameras weren't rolling, he was an intimidating figure. He was missing part of one of his middle fingers, but it didn't matter—his whole body had a way of flipping you the bird.

And he and I had to fight in this show.

A movie fight consists of throwing blows, missing by a foot, and actors snapping their heads back. But I was still kind of new to this whole movie/TV acting business. During filming, Lee and

I were throwing punches, while I was predominantly occupied with not knocking off my too-small bowler hat.

And I took one swing and hit the tip of Lee Van Cleef's nose.

Cut!

Take two! I swing again, and clipped his nose again.

Cut!!!

Take three. And my fist once again connected with Van Cleef's snout.

Let's take five!

Even though this was a few years before *The Good, the Bad and the Ugly,* I could hear the Ennio Morricone music sting as he sauntered over to me. He got right into my face, obscuring the sun and all of my hope for the future, leaned down, and growled, "If you do that again, I *will* . . . knock . . . you . . . out."

Terrifying, which brings me to one of the most important of Shatner Rules, which is . . .

RULE: Don't Punch Lee Van Cleef!

(NOTE: Lee Van Cleef died in 1989. This should probably be the easiest rule to follow.)

While in the tunnel, I figured that if I could survive my encounter with Lee Van Cleef, I could certainly survive my encounter with a wounded wild pig. I took a deep breath, steeled myself, and trudged forward.

How did I get into this situation? Well, I love Thanksgiving.

I love to say the word "Thanksgiving." It's a beautiful word and the intrinsic meaning of the word, to me, is "love." And I would be spending that Thanksgiving—the Thanksgiving of 1969—without my loved ones.

I had just divorced my wife Gloria, and she and my daughters were spending the holiday elsewhere. I would be alone. And do you know what's more terrifying to me than a wounded and angry wild boar? Being alone.

I hate being alone. I've spent most of my life filling up my existence with reservoirs of company, family around me, friends. I cherish the people I love for a variety of reasons, not the least of which is the fact that they keep me from being alone. I went through a lot of loneliness as a child, as a kid, and as a young man, and I fear it more than anything.

(NOTE: If you are seated next to William Shatner on an airplane, please be quiet. He doesn't hate being alone THAT much.)

Fortunately, a couple of days earlier, *Star Trek* cinematographer Al Francis called me and invited me over to his house for the holiday. I was thrilled. I asked, "What can I bring?" He suggested ham. And for some reason, my mind leapt to wild boar! I didn't want a piece of meat in a can you had to open with a key. I wanted a slab of meat on the hoof you had to kill with an arrow!

I must admit, for some reason Thanksgiving and danger sometimes go hand-in-hand with me. In recent years, my family has been witness to William Shatner's Thanksgiving Blastoff. And no, "blastoff" is not something having to do with bowel abnormalities. It refers to my fondness for deep-fried turkey.

Deep-fried turkey is the most delicious turkey I've ever tasted. The oil sears the skin, so the oil doesn't go into the meat. Amazing! The only problem is, the specific gravity of a turkey and the amount of oil you should have for the boiling period is never carefully calculated.

You don't want to have too little oil, because any turkey above the oil line won't cook. You've got to completely immerse the twenty-pound turkey in boiling oil, heated by an open propane flame below. So you don't want too much oil. Do you see the potential problem?

Every year I could be seen sprinting, in my shorts and sandals, away from a plume of flame, a trail of liquid fire leading to our house, my fork in one hand, oven mitt in the other.

Elizabeth eventually destroyed my deep fryer. She didn't sell it. She didn't donate it. She didn't leave it out on the curb—she destroyed it. She decided that William Shatner's Thanksgiving Blastoff would never again claim another victim with its fiery deliciousness.

So in 1969, in the fine tradition of Shatner Thanksgiving danger, I chose to hunt and kill a wild boar for the Francis family and their guests. I grabbed my bow and arrow, hired a guide, and took off to San Clemente. I noticed my guide had a .45 strapped to his side, explaining, "If things get really bad, I'll use the gun."

My guide, the expert, had a gun, and I had a bow and arrow. It then occurred to me: *What the hell am I thinking?*

Perhaps it was a control issue? My marriage had crumbled, my job had ended, and my daughters were living somewhere else.

Perhaps my desire to go out and hunt my own food was a primal urge to control my destiny, my survival. But once I got out to the island, I began to think that a safer way to act out my primitive man urges would be to rediscover fire or paint a picture of a horse on a cave wall.

So I'm trudging, and slightly trembling, around the island, and before long a massive male boar emerges from the underbrush. A giant. I pull back the string on my compound bow, aim, and release the bolt. A direct hit!

A hunting arrow works with three cutting blades, and your prey bleeds to death. You lodge an arrow into an animal, and then you don't move. You sit down and wait for an hour, for nature to take its course, for the animal to bleed out.

(NOTE: When hunting with a bow and arrow, bring a book. Or, if you have a sense of irony, a copy of Vegetarian Times.*)*

Unfortunately, no one hipped my pig to the whole "fall and slowly die" thing.

After the hit, he took off into the underbrush, my arrow in his massive flank. My guide ran after the beast. I stood there for a second, surprised, not sure what to do. It was then that I noted an entire pack of wild boar had emerged from the bushes, some even bigger than the one I hit. The guy with the .45 was gone, and I ran after him as fast as I could.

The guide came running back to me and said, "The pig went through this hole." There was a very neat—and small—tunnel in the underbrush.

He said, "I'll tell you what I'll do. I'm going to go around this brush. I'll go around and get to the other side; you go in and flush him out."

Before I could say, "Maybe I could borrow that .45 for my flushing," he was gone.

And I was crawling through the densest thicket, being pricked and poked, breathing in earthy air, my bow and arrow over my shoulder. Even if the pig did come charging after me, there would be no way to arm the bow and use it.

I was a sitting duck for a wounded pig and my goose would soon be cooked, or something like that.

Luckily, it turned out the beast had just made it out of the tunnel of brush, collapsed, and died. All my apprehension and terror was quickly replaced with the joy of the kill.

We field dressed the pig right then and there. I gave the guide a share of the meat, and headed back to Los Angeles. I dropped the kill off with Al Francis, and the wonderful and warm Mrs. Francis. Primal Shatner had hunted well.

The next day, Thanksgiving, Mrs. Francis informed me that the meat was no good. Spoiled. After I left the day before, she dutifully went to the public library and researched the proper method for preparing wild boar for consumption. Who knew the library even had a "Wild Boar Preparation and Consumption" section? She stayed up all night, taking the temperature of the flesh every two hours, bleeding it out, and to no avail. The only thing to be thankful for was that we all didn't perish from trichinosis.

I brought twenty steaks to the celebration the next day, and they were delicious. I had a wonderful time with my surrogate family.

But I couldn't help thinking about the implications of so much meat being consumed. The boar was dead, now a cow was dead. Perhaps hunting wasn't something I was entirely comfortable with? Perhaps Primal Shatner wasn't a fellow I wanted to be.

So in the 1970s, like many people, I hitched a ride to vegetarian enlightenment. I became a strict herbivore. I swore off the meat stuff. In fact, I even became a bit of an anti-meat zealot.

Vegetarian Times magazine? I was on the cover in 1983.

My interview with the magazine promoted a documentary I hosted and narrated called *The Vegetarian World*, which also featured Pulitzer Prize winner Isaac Bashevis Singer and actress Betty Buckley. In it, I espoused the virtues of such (then) exotic items as falafel and eggplant Parmesan, and solemnly declared, "Most major cities now feature several vegetarian restaurants."

And like everything I've ever done—you can watch it on You-Tube.

I could not bring the pig or the cow back, but I was going to

Bill celebrates vegetarianism, albeit briefly, in 1983.

make sure that they did not die in vain. With each Thanksgiving going forward, I would give thanks—for my enlightened sense of compassion toward all living things.

RULE: A Great Steak Trumps Good Intentions

Yes, well, I fell off the vegetarian wagon not long after I made the documentary.

Perhaps Primal Shatner will always be a part of Shatner. I no longer kill pigs for Thanksgiving, but after Elizabeth destroyed my turkey deep fryer, she bought me a very elaborate smoker and grill. I am now quite legendary around the Shatner household as an accomplished "pig butt smoker." I've been called worse.

Now my Thanksgivings are spent surrounded by loved ones, no longer alone, and thankful for a life well lived. But every year I raise a quiet toast of thanks to that mighty beast on San Clemente Island. He was a tough customer.

Not as tough as Lee Van Cleef, though. That guy still spooks me.

CHAPTER 10

RULE: If Anyone Asks You to Star in a Movie Shot Entirely in Esperanto, Say "Kiam Kaj Kiel Multa?"

That means "When, and how much?"

Yes. I starred in a feature film shot entirely in Esperanto in 1965. It was called *Incubus,* and a rather enterprising man named Leslie Stevens directed it. And by "enterprising," I mean he was a little *freneza*.

That's Esperantan for "crazy."

Esperanto was a language invented in the late 1880s by Ludwig Lazarus Zamenhof, a man who spoke Russian, Yiddish, Polish, French, Latin, Greek, Hebrew, and English, and had probably been called "smarty-pants" in each tongue. Not content with knowing every language under the sun, he invented Esperanto as a universal language to be spoken by all the world's peoples, believing that a common vocabulary would bring all the citizens of Earth together.

Well, Leslie Stevens wanted to bring all the Esperanto-speaking citizens of the world together to see a horror film shot entirely in the language, and asked me to star in it. And what's the most important of all the Shatner Rules? Even in Esperanto?

Diri jes!

Stevens created the 1960s science fiction anthology TV series *The Outer Limits.* And since it was a 1960s science fiction anthology series, I acted in it. I starred in an episode called "Cold Hands, Warm Heart," in which I played an astronaut who returned from Venus with a malady that made him cold all the time. (Nowadays, that malady is traditionally called "Being a Senior Citizen.")

FUN FACTNER: In the 1964 *Outer Limits* episode "Cold Hands, Warm Heart," William Shatner's character was involved in a mission called Project Vulcan. Isn't that weird? It totally foreshadowed his work in . . . a 1964 *Man from U.N.C.L.E.* episode called "The Project Strigas Affair." "Project" *and* "Project"? Crazy! Also, that same 1964 *Man from U.N.C.L.E.* episode that William Shatner guest-starred in also featured Leonard Nimoy. Who would later, of course, star with William Shatner in . . . an episode of *T.J. Hooker.* Weird!

RULE: Not Everything Has to Be about *Star Trek*!

Stevens started work on his script for *Incubus* after *The Outer Limits* had been canceled, and enlisted the help of cinematographer Conrad Hall, who would later win Oscars for *Butch Cassidy and the Sundance Kid*, *American Beauty*, and *Road to Perdition*. Fine films all, hampered only by their use of a language people around the world understand.

You know that language, right? English? I chose to write this book in it. Also, the copy of the *Incubus* script I got when I signed onto the project was also written in English. The contract I signed saying I would be in *Incubus*? English! The whole "shooting the film in Esperanto" thing was a secret that Leslie Stevens decided to keep to himself.

But the story spoke to me—on that level that doesn't really require a language. It was an allegorical tale in which I played a soldier arriving in a mysterious town to heal my battle wounds with the water from a miraculous spring. Demons lurked within the shadows of the village, preying on the souls of the narcissists who would exploit this fountain of youth. Kind of trippy. Watching *Incubus* might impair your ability to operate heavy machinery.

Leslie felt that the only people who needed to know about his Esperantan epic were the world's two million Esperanto speakers.

Why? Because every last one of them would buy a ticket to see this film, virtually guaranteeing a big profit!

Well, not necessarily, especially if you give the world's Esperanto speakers the shaft. Word is, some Esperantists reached out to Stevens to help with the production, and he rebuffed them. (Imagine the brief thrill some Esperantists felt when the possibility emerged that they might make some money from their ability to speak this language fluently.)

Forget the experts! Leslie Stevens alone was going to make the first movie ever shot in Esperanto—including directing the action in the language—and he was going to do this in a lightning-fast eighteen days, not including the ten days his actors had to learn their lines. Phonetically.

(NOTE: Learning . . . things . . . phone . . . et . . . i . . . cally . . . is easy . . . for . . . William . . . Shatner.)

Incubus eventually debuted at film festivals around the world. And while Esperanto speakers believe in uniting people under the banner of a common language, they aren't big believers in uniting their pals for movie night, and the film—despite some glowing reviews—quickly sank without a trace. The original print was destroyed in a fire, and it was considered a "lost" film. Most people forgot about poor, hopelessly bold and experimental *Incubus*. Except those people touched—*by its curse!*

Yes, some people believe there's a curse attached to *Incubus*.

True, some tragic elements did unfold after the film wrapped. Milos Milos, the Hungarian actor and bodyguard who played the

Incubus, died in a murder/suicide around the time of the film's release. Ann Atmar, who played my character's sister, committed suicide as well. Other actors suffered kidnappings, murders; Leslie Stevens's company went bankrupt. I promptly started on *Star Trek*.

Which—was not a curse; it was a blessing.

How did I escape the *Incubus* curse?

Well, it's complicated, but . . . I'd better write the rest of this in Esperanto.

Mi ne spektis la filmon. Ĉu vi memoras? Mi kutime ne spektas min, mi diable certe ne intencis komenci tion fari per spektado de mi dum prononcado de lingvo kiun mi ne komprenas. Kaj kelkajn monatojn post la fillmado, dum mi sidis en la ŝmink-seĝo de *Star Trek,* roko ekkraŝis tra la remorkan fenestron.

Tuj mi faris transkapiĝo-rulon (por tion fari mi ofte trovis pretekston dum la filmado de tiu filmo), senpolvigis min, kaj ekprenis la rokon. (Tuj mia dorso ekdoloriĝis, ĉar plejparte la rokoj kiujn mi kutime prenis dum *Star Trek* estis faritaj el ŝaŭmplasto.)

Doloregante, mi rimarkis noton fiksitan al la ĵetaĵo. Dum mi legis ĝin, salutis min la vortoj *"You're next, Shatner!"*

Komence mi malestime ronkis pro la uzo de

"your" anstataŭ "you're," sed tuj mi konstatis ke mi ne konis Esperanton tiom bone—eble Esperantistoj malakceptis tiun mallongigon. (Verŝajne angla-parolantoj deziras ke ankaŭ ni tion faru. Vitedas de elizioj eo ne?)

La noto ankaŭ klarigis ke La Esperantistoj koleris ĉar oni ne konsultis ilin dum la filmado, kaj ĉar oni ne invitis ilin al la premiero. Krome, kelkaj aŭtograf-petoj ĉe mia oficejo restis neresponditaj. Iuokaze, la Esperantistoj decidis malbeni *Incubus* kaj iun kiu spektis la filmon.

(NOTO: Verŝajne la filmon oni plej varme akceptis kaj spektis en Francio. Tie malbenoj ne estas granda afero. Fakte, francoj ja pasas la plej grandan parton de la vivo ĉirkaŭataj de francoj!)

Mi decidis mem detrui ĉiun ekzempleron de *Incubus* kiun mi povos trovi. Dum breĉo de la filmo. Serioze, mi ne intencis rapidigi ĉi tiun aferon. Ĉar kiel malicaj povus esti la Esperantistoj? Ili devontigis sin al monda paco per la komuneco de lingvoj.

Kaj dum pasis tempo, mi informiĝis ke fluaj parolantoj de Klingon estas multe pli granda manpleno . . . Ĉiuokaze, reirante al la angla . . .

FUN FACTNER: If you want to know what William Shatner just said, go to William Shatner.com.

After being lost for many years, a print of *Incubus* was found in France (of course) in 1999. The SyFy Channel restored it and released it on DVD. Mo Rocca of *The Daily Show with Jon Stewart* on Comedy Central interviewed me at the time, heralding me as a "great foreign film actor" and "the top Esperanto box office draw." *(NOTE TO SELF: Update business cards.)*

Rocca also had a focus group of Esperanto speakers watch the film, who had unkind things to say about my Esperantan pronunciations.

Well, to them I say, "Kiss my butt."

(That's actually the same in Esperanto as it is in English. We are all of us, in the world, united by certain commonalities.)

QUIZ

Which celebrity did not attended the premiere of *Incubus* at the San Francisco Film Festival in 1966?

A. Roman Polanski

B. Sharon Tate

C. William Shatner

C. William Shatner. I had something else going on. And judging from the fact that the curse might have extended itself to the people who did attend, I consider myself lucky.

CHAPTER 11

RULE: Balls Are Important, but Stones Are Money

M y wife and I were in New York to attend a black-tie charity gala a few years ago. We were both dressed to kill, but a sudden, sharp pain in my side felt as if someone were killing me.

So I wound up in the hospital, in my tuxedo, on a weekend evening. Have you ever been inside an emergency room? In New York City? On a weekend? I don't remember the name of said hospital, but from the looks of things that night, it was somewhere in the outer borough of Despair.

The emergency room was so crowded, in fact, that I was not admitted to a proper room with a proper bed, but stuck on a gurney in a dark hallway. The gurney had stirrups, and in my sufferings, I stuck my feet in them to take some of the weight off my nether regions. My eyes were closed tight with the blinding pain, but I remember distinctly at one point a female passing me and saying, "Look, Captain Kirk is having a baby!"

RULE: When Insulting William Shatner, Don't Be Afraid to Dig a Little Deeper into the Résumé. Even in Great Pain, He Will Appreciate the Effort of a *TekWar* or *Kingdom of the Spiders* Reference.

Yep, the doctor said I had a kidney stone, and there was nothing to do but wait for it to pass. And take morphine. One, two, three shots of exquisite relief. Feeling no pain, I was now ready to go and hit the gala, but the wife wisely suggested that we stay in, and await the glorious arrival of my tiny bundle of uric acid and/or calcium buildup.

All things must pass, and my stone was no exception. It left fairly painlessly, we headed back home to Los Angeles, and for a few years my kidneys dutifully sorted waste products from my blood without incident.

Then, in 2006 . . .

Denny Crane was bent over Candice Bergen's desk, in a swirling maelstrom of physical agony.

(NOTE: This is not a passage from some kind of depraved Boston Legal *fan fiction one would find on the Internet. Characters I've played, for some reason or other, always wind up in the most licentious fantasies of fan fiction authors. For years now, Kirk and Spock have heated up the pages of the fan fiction subgenre known as slash fiction, which deals primarily in gay relationships. Neither of us is homosexual, but if I were to dabble, I would surely avoid any encounter with a creature famed for its Vulcan death grip.)*

(ADDITIONAL NOTE: I have also been informed that there is more than one webpage out there dedicated to Denny Crane/Alan Shore slash fiction. It must have been all the cigar smoking we did. Either way, the fair-haired dazzlement that is James Spader is a bit more appealing than Spock. Sorry, Leonard.)

(FINAL NOTE: And it has come to my attention that some enterprising web scribes have also published **T.J. Hooker** *slash fiction. I guess I had a way with a nightstick.)*

(ADDENDUM TO FINAL NOTE: Please, slash fiction writers, don't ever write any **Twilight Zone** *"Nightmare at 20,000 Feet" stories. (I'd hate to picture myself making love to a gremlin.)*

Let us return to a subject slightly more savory: my agony. I was there on the set, collapsed on my costar's desk, bellowing, writhing, and flailing my arms about. For some, such histrionics are the universal signal that "Shatner's acting again," but eventually I was able to convince the crew and the producers that I was in pain and needed medical attention. I was carted off from the set in an ambulance.

(Keep in mind, in the four seasons of *Boston Legal*, more than twenty different actors were hired to play recurring characters on the show, and many were fired after a season as David E. Kelly tinkered with the program's formula. Dramatic exits on that set were the norm, but since I didn't have a cardboard box of my belongings on my belly as I lay on the stretcher, people assumed I would be coming back.)

My body had manufactured more kidney stones. I was taken to a hospital in Burbank, where I was refused painkillers until the doctor examined me. I was desperate for them, and I pleaded for a doctor, any doctor—Dr. Scholl, Dr. Pepper, anyone—to hit me with that morphine syringe.

No dice—I had to wait in an agony akin to the kind experienced by the crew of the Starship *Enterprise* when they were forced to wear the collars of obedience in the episode "The Gamesters of Triskelion."

> **RULE:** *TekWar* and *Kingdom of the Spiders*——While Esoteric——Sometimes Won't Give You the Reference You Need

Eventually, it became clear that this latest stone had no intention of going peacefully like its predecessor. It was not going to walk out of me with its hardened, crystallized hands in the air. The doctors were going to have to go in.

We were going to go . . . where no man . . . should go . . . at all.

The probe went up my urethra like Marlow trekking up the Congo to retrieve Kurtz in Joseph Conrad's *Heart of Darkness*. (By the way, high school students, feel free to use this analogy in any paper you might be required to write on Conrad's seminal work. *A* for originality!)

And they produced from my insides a little black crystal, a diabolic diamond, an onyx of agony. Forged in the heat of my body, compressed in my mighty urethra.

> **RULE: In the Shatnerverse, Even the Surgical Procedure of Ureteroscopy Demands Dramatic Flourish!**

I could now put my kidney stone behind me, and return to a normal life.

Oh, did I mention I'm William Shatner? A "normal life" is sometimes just out of my grasp, which I was reminded of when I got the phone call from GoldenPalace.com.

Golden Palace is an online casino, run out of the Kahnawake Mohawk Territory near my beloved Montreal. When they aren't separating Internet gambling addicts from their hard-earned money with online blackjack, the people at Golden Palace engage in all sorts of bizarre publicity stunts. They once purchased a ten-year-old grilled cheese sandwich with an image of the Virgin Mary burned into the toast for $28,000. Did they eat it? I mean, talk about Immaculate Indigestion.

Golden Palace is the company that had their logo painted on Danny Bonaduce's back when he participated in the reality show *Celebrity Boxing.* They are the company that sponsored the work of professional streaker Mark Roberts. (How much overhead does a streaker need to cover?) They even paid a woman $15,000 to get their logo tattooed on her forehead.

They obviously wanted to class up their image a bit by getting into the business of William Shatner's urethra. Golden Palace reached out to me with an offer of $25,000 for my kidney stone.

The whole thing struck me as rather distasteful. And insulting.

Only $25,000? I won't get out of bed for that kind of money, and I certainly won't lie down in a gurney with my feet in stirrups for it. My kidney stone was a precious and pure calcification of magic publicity. It was time to do what I do best:

Negotiate!

My counteroffer was $100,000. This was a genuine William Shatner kidney stone. It conceivably could have been the most famous kidney stone extracted in the world; $25,000 was a pittance for my pain and suffering. If I were to settle for such a paltry amount—forget GOLDEN PALACE; they could tattoo SUCKER on my forehead.

And not just *my* pain and suffering—there was Elizabeth's suffering, the suffering of the *Boston Legal* crew, and the suffering of Candice Bergen to think about.

FUN FACTNER: One of Candice Bergen's first films was *The Sand Pebbles*, which was also my nickname for my kidney stones.

Perhaps it was the mental duress imposed upon this five-time Emmy-winning actress that touched the hearts of the folks at Golden Palace, because they came around to offering $75,000 for my kidney stone. And since I had no plans to save the stone and press it into the pages of a scrapbook, or mount it onto a ring for my wife, I accepted the offer, and pledged to give the money to charity.

And Golden Palace could do with the stone what they wanted. I'm sure it tasted better than a ten-year-old grilled cheese Virgin Mary relic.

The *Boston Legal* family also kicked in an additional $25,000, and I donated the money to Habitat for Humanity. Such is the power of saying "yes!" (Seriously, remember that rule the next time an online casino wants to pay you for your kidney stones. You'll thank me.)

Habitat for Humanity is an international nonprofit organization devoted to building homes for the people without the means to buy one. They are located in Atlanta, Georgia, and in 2006, they were busy helping rebuild after the carnage of Katrina. Our $100,000 was used to build a home in Louisiana for a family who had been displaced by the storm. My kidney stone, more viable than Freddie Mac or Countrywide, built a wonderful, lovely home. It was worth all that pain and humiliation.

I was later blessed with a photo of the house that my kidney stone built, and the smiling Louisiana family out front. I have never spoken to them, but perhaps this is a good time to explain to them some of the . . .

RULES FOR LIVING IN THE HOUSE THAT SHATNER'S KIDNEYS BUILT

1. If Shatner ever comes by, he gets to use the bathroom.
2. As a sign of tribute, please rename your home Billstone Manor. I can provide you with my measurements for the statue out front. (They won't be exactly accurate—the statue might be made a little taller and more ripped—but this is a *tribute*.)
3. If Shatner does come by, please provide fresh water and foods that are not high in oxalate. I know you like your home, but I never want to get kidney stones again.

QUIZ

Which type of kidney stones did William Shatner suffer from?

A. Calcium oxalate stones

B. Calcium phosphate stones

C. Uric acid stones

D. Struvite stones

E. Cystine stones

F. All of the above

The answer is B, calcium phosphate stones. If anyone tries to sell you some authentic William Shatner struvite stones or genuine Shatner cystine rocks, they are ripping you off! And if you gleefully answered "all of the above," you're some kind of sick sadist!

CHAPTER 12

RULE: You Can Always Find a Good Friend in a White Crowd

U m, you know, that rule didn't come out quite right.

(It sounds like something my character, Adam Cramer, would have said in the 1962 Roger Corman ahead-of-its-time racial drama *The Intruder*. Haven't seen it? You should. It really holds up.)

Now where was I? Oh yes, I was offering up a non-racist rule.

RULE, TAKE TWO: Never Wear White after Labor Day. Or Any Day until the Following Labor Day.

That's a little better. Now, this story—like all great stories—starts with Marjoe Gortner.

Remember Marjoe Gortner? He first came to fame as a child evangelist and faith healer, and at four years old was touted as "the youngest ordained minister in history." He was the subject of the 1972 Academy Award–winning documentary *Marjoe,* in which he revealed some of the more lucrative—and fraudulent—aspects of the tent revival business.

Marjoe parlayed this fame into an acting career, where he played a psychotic thug in the movie *Earthquake*, a psychotic thug in *When You Comin' Back, Red Ryder?*, and a psychotic thug in the acclaimed TV movie *The Marcus-Nelson Murders*, which also introduced the world to a detective named Kojak, played by Telly Savalas. Clearly, if you can convince people you speak to God, you can also convince them you are psychotic.

Marjoe and I starred together in a TV movie in the 1970s called *Pray for the Wildcats*, in which Andy Griffith played the psychotic thug. (There's a change of pace.) And we've remained friendly ever since. Marjoe is a unique guy and somewhat difficult to cast, so he has since retired from the movie bad guy game and now organizes great charity sporting events around the country and the world. And I was lucky enough to be invited to one in Jamaica a few years back.

My wife and I landed on the lush island paradise and checked into our suite. It was very nicely appointed, and on the bureau was a beautifully engraved invitation to a "White Party" the following evening. I must admit to being somewhat flummoxed by the invitation, and saddened to see the last vestiges of colonialism still hanging on. The missus then attempted to assuage my fears by telling me it was a party in which all the attendees were to *wear* white. My fears were only assuaged somewhat.

Sorry, but I don't wear all-white ensembles, and certainly don't travel around with them.

Why? Well, I've been away from my hometown of Montreal

for many years, but a bit of my hometown of Montreal goes with me wherever I go. It's freezing there. The only people who wear all white in that city are the asylum orderlies whose job it is to collect people in Montreal who wear all white. You do not walk around in the City of Saints dressed for the tropics.

FUN FACTNER: Montreal is sometimes called the City of Saints, in case you were wondering where I got that.

I shrugged it off. I had some white socks. That ought to count for something. Who was going to be so uptight as to deny me admittance to a party because of a lack of foresight when packing my suitcase?

The wife would.

> **RULE: Anything Can Be Negotiated——As Long as You're Not Negotiating with Your Wife**

Mrs. Shatner had an all-white ensemble and was determined that the two of us were going to attend this lovely beach party together, no matter what. And apparently, my white birthday suit would not be appropriate. It was not *that* kind of beach.

I then dragged said lily-white self into the soak tub to contemplate this sartorial conundrum. I guess I could *buy* a white suit or something, just to attend a party for a few hours, and then maybe I could return it? Hopefully with a minimum of curry goat or jerk chicken stains? That seemed like an awful bother, I thought to myself, as I gently batted around the rubber duck. (I do pack the *important* things.)

Then I looked around the bathroom and saw the answer to my problem . . . hanging on the back of the door.

My wife made sure she walked several paces ahead of me as we made our way to the all-white beach party later that night. I sauntered behind her, resplendent in my white socks, white tennis shoes, and . . . white terrycloth hotel bathrobe. And while I'm not a man who likes to share the color of his underwear, let's just say I was following the dress code to a T, or, more precisely, a BVD.

Of course, the whole event was a deliriously fun bacchanalia. Marjoe is a larger-than-life personality and a delightful host. Who would have thought that a guy who grew up handling snakes and speaking in tongues would throw such great parties? And the way some folk were drinking, they would probably need his old faith healing skills first thing in the morning.

My improvised ensemble was a big hit, and decidedly more in keeping with the whole vibe of Jamaica. (In fact, many asked me if I was stoned.) It was a wonderful night with wonderful people but then . . . something horrible caught my eye.

I saw someone across the sand. Another partygoer. Someone doing the one thing no Hollywood celebrity ever wants to see!

He was wearing my outfit.

My exact same outfit!

It was a red carpet emergency, or, in this case, a white sand debacle!

FUN FACTNER: William Shatner always carries his T.J. Hooker nightstick with him on the red carpet. It's the only way to keep Joan Rivers in line.

Someone else had the audacity to show up in white tennis shoes, white socks, and a gigantic, fluffy hotel bathrobe. Stealing *my* look! I stomped over to see who else dared wave the terrycloth banner of good times.

It was Olympic gold medalist Scott Hamilton, of course.

I confronted him; we both started laughing, and hit it off immediately. Turns out the 1984 gold medal Olympian for figure skating didn't bring an all-white outfit to Jamaica. Why?

He's a figure skater.

It's cold on ice. It's cold in Montreal. People who spend that much time in the cold just don't *do* beach attire.

So I went to a party, risked the possibility of great ridicule, and by the end of it had made a great friend. So, wear a bathrobe to your next important event and tell them you are just following the lessons of William Shatner. (They might get peeved if your next important event is a funeral, though.)

Shatner Gets Serious

All kidding aside, I love Scott, and we have remained great friends to this day. His ability to overcome hardship is one of his many strengths. As a child, he suffered a growth disorder, and he overcame it to become an Olympian and a gold medalist. And now he is a cancer survivor who—even after having a benign brain tumor removed—can still do a backflip on skates. Nowadays, he heads up the Scott Hamilton CARES Initiative, an advocacy group working hard to find a cure for the disease. Every year he raises money with the Scott Hamilton Ice Show and Gala, a black tie event. Or, in Scott's and my case, a "black-robe soiree."

CHAPTER 13

RULE: Know When to Turn Shatner On, and When to Turn Shatner Off

kay, this rule has nothing to do with sex. If it did, why would I start off by writing . . .

DÜSSELDORF

ESSEN

FRANKFURT

NUREMBERG?

Yes, nothing says "sexy" like the names of German cities, and a few years back I was zipping by them while driving 135 mph on the Autobahn. (Keep in mind, I was wearing my seatbelt while driving at 135 mph, so in case I got into an accident, I would be trisected into three neat sections. That would make for easier cleanup; truly, the German way.)

Not only do I find Germany unsexy, but I also find it unsettling. Why?

RULE: Never Watch the History Channel before Visiting Germany

Please don't take it personally, Germany, but the little Jewish kid inside of me from Montreal who grew up during World War II just doesn't like the sound of Düsseldorf, Essen, Frankfurt, and Nuremberg.

FUN FACTNER: William Shatner was in the film *Judgment at Nuremberg* along with Spencer Tracy, Burt Lancaster, Richard Widmark, Judy Garland, Marlene Dietrich, and Montgomery Clift. The film won two Academy Awards.*

* ADDENDUM TO PREVIOUS FUN FACTNER: The above Fun Factner is the only "fun" fact ever associated with Nuremberg.

The trunk of my rental car was filled with everything I'd need to put myself at ease in Germany: several pairs of lederhosen and a return-trip ticket. I was really questioning my decision to visit, but I was in Germany because of that most important Shatner Rule: Say "ja!"

I had been asked to appear at an event for German television, along with that other famed German television icon: Charlton Heston. We were both receiving some kind of lifetime achievement award.

Charlton Heston was a fine actor and a movie icon, but I didn't know the man and was really looking forward to meeting him. I am drawn to controversial figures, and in recent years Heston had grown more and more political and—to some people—a little polarizing. The man had played Moses, but he was currently a God to gun owners across America.

FUN FACTNER: Both Charlton Heston and William Shatner served as Bacchus King at Mardi Gras. Only one of them had the courage to go pantsless.

This was around the time Charlton Heston was standing before NRA gatherings, raising a musket in his hand, and bellowing, *"From my cold dead hands!"* Since he was joining me for this event in Germany, I could only assume he softened that stance when passing through airport security.

Before our awards show, I was to meet Heston in person, as we were both going to be guests of honor at a dinner for the event advertisers at a German restaurant. Although if we were really guests of honor, they would have taken us somewhere besides a German restaurant.

One German horror *not* chronicled by the History Channel is the food. To be fair, around this time, I had become a bit of a food snob, having just come off hosting *Iron Chef USA*. We had shot two specials, featuring myself and celebrity judges Steve Schirripa, Brande Roderick, and comedy writer and *Hollywood Squares* fixture Bruce Vilanch.

And by the way—if you're going to have Bruce Vilanch on a cooking show, expect one or more hairs in your food.

It was similar to the popular Japanese program, except now *I* was the chairman, swaggering around Kitchen Stadium in what can best be described as an "Edwardian spacesuit," lording over such contests as "Dungeness Crab Challenge!" In fact, my experience on *Iron Chef USA* brought across my palate a dessert concoction that celebrity chef Kerry Simon called Crab Gelato. It was an ice cream that was the true essence of crab!

Was it the essence of *good*?

Well, I was relieved not to see it on our menu that evening at the German restaurant. And Simon was in tears when the judges on *Iron Chef USA* spat it into their napkins.

FUN FACTNER: After doing *Iron Chef USA*, William Shatner cooked Kentucky burgoo on a television show called *Cooking's a Drag*, featuring a sassy transvestite chef named Betty Dee Lishous. Mr. Shatner no longer does cooking programs.

As soon as Elizabeth and I arrived at the restaurant, I was introduced to Mr. Heston, and he was . . . a little chilly. Somewhat aloof. Occasionally, those of us who have plied our trade in television get a bit of the cold shoulder from the actors who have spent most of their careers on the big(ger) screen. Although I'm not sure if he was being distant or just being . . . Charlton Heston: square-jawed, iconic, ready to remove damned dirty ape hands from his person at a moment's notice.

Which brings me to my rule: When I'm not being Shatner, I turn it off.

Depending on the location, when you meet me, you probably won't meet Shatner. I will probably be in Bill mode. Bill's a very nice guy. He likes horses, and his kids and grandkids. Bill adores his wife. Bill turns the lights off at night and makes sure the bills get paid, and he memorizes his lines during his spare time so he doesn't get fired from his current job. That's who Bill is. (He tries not to speak of himself in the third person, but sometimes it just slips through.)

The real William Shatner is a fairly decaffeinated version of the one you see on TV. I can't keep that energy, that intensity, up all the time. I am not even allowed to drink caffeine. Elizabeth's efforts to keep caffeinated beverages out of my hands are sometimes tantamount to spousal abuse.

> **RULE: Mention Spousal Abuse in Any Autobiographical Work. It'll Help Sell Some Copies.**

William Shatner—as you have hopefully learned by now—is a bit of a character. But I'm not the William Shatner character. I'm not the hyper, arrogant, bombastic fellow people are laughing along with. (You're laughing *with* him, not *at him*, right?) When we meet, I will not lace my fingers together and club you like Kirk, I will not ride on the hood of your car like Hooker, and I will not try and sell you the best deal possible on airfares and hotels like The Negotiator.*

Unless, of course, you like saving money! Do I have some deals for you!

Besides, it's hard for me to be Shatneresque because . . . well, how do I put this in a "Shatneresque" way?

I . . .

Don't . . .

Watch . . .

Myself.

Yep. When Shatner comes on the TV, Bill changes the channel. I have spent a huge part of my life in the public eye. Everybody's public eyes but my own.

I have never felt comfortable watching myself. I didn't do it early in my career, and I don't do it now. I don't like watching my work, or the work of that old devil, Time. On the occasions when I have directed myself in something, when my face appears in the dailies, I actually raise a hand to block out my face. I also can usually find some fault with my performances. My toughest critic is me, but fortunately he doesn't watch me and attack me in the press.

Upon meeting Heston, I realized he was one of those guys who didn't have an Off switch. And I, and my dinner companions, became acutely aware of this after our main course.

We were all full of sauerbraten, knockwurst, pretzels of the hardest variety, and Gaisburger Marsch. (No idea. I wished it tasted as good as crab gelato.) We had met all the advertising folk; I tried to be my best charming Bill, hobnobbing with the German TV execs, and now all there was to do was eat dessert.

Heston pushed his chair back and stood, cleared his mighty throat, and declared, "I suppose you would all like to hear me recite some passages from the Bible."

Before any of us could get out a "*nein*," Heston leapt into a performance of the Bible. He was "Bible acting."

I know "Bible acting." I did quite a bit of it when I was a young actor. There was a weekly TV show called *Lamp unto My Feet*. I acted on the Sunday morning religious anthology *Insight*. I was in several episodes of a program called *The Psalms* in 1962, which was shot by a young cameraman by the name of George Lucas. (This was before we both discovered the joys of galaxies far, far away.)

RULE: Always Be Nice to Your Cameraman

"Bible acting" involves speaking in very soft, rounded, accent-free tones. It is quiet, hushed. Words are spoken with great reverence. You must act in a way that suggests you are deathly afraid of waking up the nearby Baby Jesus. And this is what Heston was doing.

For about thirty minutes.

"Begat this, begat that, begat whatshisname."

There I was, a Jew in Germany, stuffed with brats, getting the full God treatment from Moses. Heston went Old Testament, he went New Testament, no one went to the bathroom. We just sat there, frozen, unsure of what to do or say. How do you stand up and say, "Hey, Charlton Heston, let's cut to Revelations so we can all get our strudel"?

You can't, of course. He's Charlton Heston, and he's being Charlton Heston.

What's the lesson? You have to be able to *turn it off*. For your sake, and for the sake of your dinner companions.

EPILOGUE

The event was great, and both Heston and I wowed the German TV audience. At least I think they were wowed, although when I ordered them all to march into Poland they seemed a little dumbfounded. (I guess charisma only gets you so far in Germany these days.)

When I got home, there was a bill waiting for me from my German hotel. I had spilled a glass of red wine on my room's white carpet, and the hotel was attempting to charge me $40,000! I told them I was Bill, and that they should send the damage fees to William Shatner.

I hear he can negotiate his way out of anything.

CHAPTER 14

RULE: Grab Life by the (Golden) Throat!

Two men sat in my Ventura Boulevard office one morning. They called themselves the Foos Brothers. And no, they didn't appear to be a vaudeville act.

They were nice enough fellows, we shared a few laughs and pleasantries, but I wasn't quite sure . . . who they were. My ubiquitous presence on the media landscape is the result of projects that stem from many meetings such as these, and sometimes I get people mixed up.

They had a pitch of some sort. I listened politely while craning my neck to get a look at my daily planner. The day was, as usual, very full, and the word "Rhino" was filled in between 10 and 11 A.M. I like rhinos. In fact, there's a picture of me riding a rhino in my office. What a great day that was when I met the rhino—I also got to swim with an orca and hold some cheetah kittens. Around 1987? My mind was drifting as the Foos boys were pitching; I looked at my rhino picture, and smiled.

Again, very nice young men, but what did they want—?

A record.

They wanted me to record an album. They *used* to be with Rhino Records, and now they had a new label called Shout! Factory.

Now, Rhino *was* familiar. What did they do . . . ?

Golden Throats.

Oh no. The guys who produced *Golden Throats* were in my office, asking me to make a record. Perhaps this could be a perfect opportunity to wring *their* golden throats?

For the uninitiated, *Golden Throats* was a series of compilation albums released starting in 1988, which featured cover songs performed by people who were not known as traditional singers. Among the highlights: Eddie *"Green Acres"* Albert's take on Bob Dylan's "Blowin' in the Wind," Mae West singing "Twist and Shout" at an age when she could barely do either, *Dragnet's* Jack Webb doing a "just the facts" rendition of "Try a Little Tenderness," and Leonard Nimoy hammering away at "If I Had a Hammer" and "Proud Mary."

Leonard was one of two artists featured on the album twice. The other was me.

My renditions of "Lucy in the Sky with Diamonds" and "Mr. Tambourine Man"—from my 1968 album, *The Transformed Man*—were highlighted on *Golden Throats*. Being highlighted on that album was not a tribute; it was a form of mockery. Needless to say, *Golden Throats* is *not* on my iPod. For one thing, I'd have to know how to put things on my iPod.

I let these Foos chat on, aware that their intentions for me were probably not the best. I sent my assistant down to the corner for coffee and gave her the wink, which was the signal for "put something nasty in their cups."

I clasped my hands behind my head, and let my mind wander again, back many years ago, to the release of *The Transformed Man.*

> **RULE: When Writing a Lengthy Account of Your Musical Career, Alert the Reader to the Presence of a Flashback so They Don't Get Confused. . . .**

> **FLASHBACK!**

Sometime in 1968, Fred de Cordova, the executive producer of a famous late night television show, looked at me, shook his head, and said, "Three minutes."

I pled, "But the song is six minutes."

"It's two songs," he insisted, "Do one or the other. If I were you, I'd do the Dylan number. The kids like that."

My rehearsal for an appearance on *The Tonight Show Starring Johnny Carson* had just ended, and we had run through the second track of side one of my album, which was "Theme from Cyrano/ Mr. Tambourine Man." On that tune, I read a poem from Rostand's *Cyrano de Bergerac* in which "I may climb to no great heights, but I will climb alone" dovetails into Dylan's song, which I performed as a drug addict hungry for a fix.

Sound heady? It *was* heady! It was 1968!

It was the year the Beatles visited the Maharishi, it was the year *Hair* opened, side 2 of the Velvet Underground's *White Light/White Heat* album featured the seventeen-minute-long "Sister Ray," the Amboy Dukes took us on a "Journey to the Center of the Mind," Richard Harris's seven-minute-long "MacArthur Park" went to number two, Iron Butterfly released the eighteen-minute-long "In-A-Gadda-Da-Vida." Our minds were expanding, and so was our patience for long, freaky pop numbers. And I wanted to be as long and freaky as the rest of them.

Come on! Six minutes of William Shatner was nothing compared to eighteen minutes of Iron Butterfly, but Fred de Cordova wouldn't hear of it. I could do Rostand or Dylan, but not both.

How dare you, Mr. de Cordova? I was a musician! And I had the concept album to prove it.

And it's not like I had never sung on a talk show. Earlier in the year, I had broken out into song on *The Mike Douglas Show*, singing a tune called "Keep It Gay."

FUN FACTNER: While it means something completely different today, in the 1960s, "gay" meant "happy," "cheery," "full of merriment," and "homosexual."

It was a great performance. In fact, if you type "William Shatner" and "Keep It Gay" into YouTube, you can watch the clip.

RULE: In Whatever Way You Can, Help Shatner Destroy YouTube

I tried to explain to Fred what I was attempting to do with *The Transformed Man,* which was link great literature of the past with great modern literature—the poetry found in many songs of the sixties. Taking one song out of context would destroy the connection. Elsewhere on the album, I paired Hamlet with Sinatra, "Lucy in the Sky with Diamonds" with a poem called "Spleen." It all made sense in context.

Can you dig it, Fred de Cordova?!?!

But my pleas fell on deaf—and hopelessly square—ears. De Cordova, not digging it and in a hurry to oversee the wrapping of Johnny's Carnac the Magnificent turban, told me, "Do the Dylan number. Nobody knows the Cyrano thing."

So I did "Mr. Tambourine Man" as a junkie, and my allotted

three minutes didn't allow me to outline some of the headier concepts presented in *The Transformed Man* to the millions of people watching *The Tonight Show*. I was uncertain, but I performed it like only I can.

As I worked my way through the number, I eventually collapsed to the ground, in front of Doc Severinsen and the Tonight Show Band, looked heavenward, and screamed, *"MR. TAMBOU-RINE MAAAAAANNNN!"*

I finished, turned toward Johnny, and saw him mouth the words, "What . . . the . . . fuck?"

It seems most of America mouthed those words as well. That was the beginning of the end of *The Transformed Man*, an album frequently mocked, but one I am proud of. It vanished pretty quickly, and I moved on. And then . . .

Golden Throats came out. It all came rushing back to the pop culture landscape.

Which brings me back to my meeting with the ex–Rhino Records executives. They continued on about how great it would be for me to record another album with them, how they would enlist their full support, shoot videos, blah, blah, blah. These guys were just looking for a gag version of *The Transformed Man*, and I wanted no part of it.

My album became a joke to many people, and for better or worse I had learned to go along with the joke as time went by, but . . . no thanks. I was ready to show the Foos boys the door when . . .

I got a phone call. It was Ben.

Ben whatshisname.

FUN FACTNER: William Shatner can never remember the last name of his good friend and frequent collaborator Ben Folds.

Ben Folds! Yes. Ben Folds was on the line! Right in the middle of my meeting with Shout! Factory.

Full disclosure: I can never remember Ben Folds's last name. The only way I can is by applying a methodology, a mnemonic, in which I bend myself in the middle, creating a folding action after Ben's name. I suit the action to the word—it's the same way you act Shakespeare! So needless to say, I will be folding myself over as I write the rest of this book whenever Ben's surname comes up.

Ben (fold) Folds is a wonderful singer and songwriter from North Carolina, a beloved figure in the world of alternative pop, and a longtime fan of . . . *The Transformed Man.* When he picked it up at a garage sale as a kid, he had never seen Johnny Carson and had not yet heard of *Golden Throats.* He was a fan of Captain Kirk and his rather wild and strange record album. And in 1998, he asked me to provide some vocals on his record *Fear of Pop.* I had heard of his music, loved it, and agreed.

RULE: If You Want to Seem Rock-and-Roll, Don't Admit That You Had Never Heard of Ben Folds and Consented to Do It Only Because Your Daughter Told You To

So out of the blue—in the middle of my meeting with the Foos boys—Ben calls me. I spoke to him briefly, didn't quite listen to what he said, but then looked up at the record execs, and declared, "I'll do a record, but only with Ben Folds."

The Fooses (Foosi?) almost spat out their coffee—and agreed right there on the spot.

Within a couple of weeks, I had traveled to Nashville to meet with Ben. Tucked under my arm were fifty sets of lyrics I had composed. Before I knew it, I was there, ready to rock, and waiting for Joe Jackson to finish his warm-ups.

They took a very long time.

CHAPTER 15

RULE: Respect the Artistic Process of Others, Even If Their Process Takes Forever

Yes, I'll never forget the day that Ben (fold) Folds introduced me to British musician and singer-songwriter Joe Jackson. It was kind of a long day. He and I were to perform a cover of Pulp's "Common People" for my new album, *Has Been.*

We came up with the title for the album after I was at an industry event and a young actress refused to take a photo with me, declaring, "No, I don't wanna take a picture with him. Not that has-been."

Charming. This made me long for the warmth of Charlton Heston.

What does that mean, anyway? *Has-been?* If I still "am," I "be." Correct? And if I "were," at least I "was." Right? "Was" means I got "there"! In Hollywood, "there" is the goal! And as far as I and many of my fans are concerned, I still "is"! That actress, no doubt, was new to there—Hollywood—and who knows if she still is? I no longer remember her. Where is she "be"? But I digress.

Anyway, we thought it was the perfect title, and Ben then chose a cast of perfect collaborators with whom I could create this album.

Jackson floated in all the way from England, although I understand nowadays he lives in Berlin. I think the Germans keep the white, white Joe Jackson around so that they might feel "ethnic." He is a white wraith, with white-blonde hair, tall and thin and ephemeral. He was in a cloud. He reminded me of Nosferatu, and I half expected all the flowers in Nashville to shrivel and wilt in his wake.

He came into the studio and plopped down in front of a piano in the sound booth. And began to warm up. He would make . . . sounds. Tinkle away at keys. Make more sounds. Tinkle. Sounds. Tinkle. Sounds.

For three hours.

At one point, I walked up to the window in the sound booth and took a look at him. As with Ben, my daughters were very helpful in letting me know Mr. Jackson's story. He emerged as a force in the British punk/New Wave movement in the late 1970s, where he created a sound that was an eclectic hybrid of pop, classical, and jazz. It was really a thrill to work with him, especially after I realized that the Joe Jackson who Ben kept talking about was not the patriarch of the Jackson 5. I'm not sure I could have taken that kind of trauma.

I watched Joe do his warm-ups and gave him a little wave. Joe looked up from what he was doing, rose, floated out of the booth, and had a conference with Ben.

Ben later called me over and said, "Joe doesn't want you to look at him."

Oooookaaayyy. Joe seemed to be taking a page from the actress who didn't want to be photographed with me. I thought my transition to rock star was going to award me the slavish devotion that would entitle me to a rock star–sized ego. Either way, I respected the man's process, backed off, and let him enter into hour four of his warm-ups unwatched.

The warm-ups were worth it. Joe Jackson's vocals on "Common People" are enough to send shivers down your spine. (Although honestly, a lot about Joe Jackson is a tad spine-tingling.) All the people I worked with on that record were great: Aimee Mann, Brad Paisley, and Henry Rollins, who I've stayed friends with ever since. Henry and I performed a song called "I Can't Get Behind That," which featured him and me trading shouts over a freight train of percussion and guitar feedback. That performance certainly would have harshed the mellow of my "Mr. Tambourine Man" junkie.

Rollins has released many spoken-word records, so pairing up with the world's premier "speak-singer" was a natural for me. Also, I like to stand next to him to appear more buff. Seriously, Henry— hit the gym!

> **RULE: Make Cracks about Henry Rollins When He Is a Good Distance Away**

FUN FACTNER: Henry Rollins was once the manager of a Häagen-Dazs store in the Georgetown neighborhood of Washington, D.C. And he's the only guy on Earth who can say "white chocolate raspberry truffle" and still sound tough.

Ben and I learned a lot from one another making this record. He helped shape my fifty different sets of lyrics into cohesive songs. At first, though, he was surprised I came in with anything.

"I figured we would just write them here," he said.

"Wait a minute. You mean you don't have the written material, like a script, when you come into the studio?" said I, incredulous.

"No, we never do that. We just make it up as we go along."

I guess that's rock and roll, but that's an anathema to me. I don't "wing it." I'm a stickler for "process" when it comes to performing. When I act, I don't use understudies, I do all my own camera rehearsals, and I am never late. I never arrive without all my lines learned. And I showed up to Nashville with my fifty sets of lyrics, ready to work.

First thing in the morning.

Which for Ben, was around 11:30.

> **RULE: Don't Assume It's Ben Folds Five. More Like Seven or Eight, If You're Lucky.**

Ben was very rock-and-roll. When he said to arrive at 11 A.M., I would be waiting for a half hour to an hour. Eventually, I had to have a sit-down with him. We were paying for the studio space— why waste it? Being on a schedule is very un-rock-and-roll, but being not rock-and-roll is the most rock-and-roll thing you can do, right? I was totally being rock-and-roll with my un-rock-and-rollness.

Ben and I learned a lot from one another. He taught me about music, about the power of collaboration, about telling the truth with my lyrics. I like to think I taught him about the little hand and big hand on the clock. We put together a great album—in two weeks. And have maintained a friendship ever since.

Before long, we were performing together in support of the album, even appearing on *The Tonight Show with Jay Leno*, which by then had been Fred de Cordova–free for many years. After we performed "Common People," no one was mouthing "what the fuck?"

We played the entire album, with a full band, including Joe Jackson and Henry Rollins, at the historic El Rey Theatre in Los

Angeles. "El rey" means "the king," and I certainly felt like royalty in front of the eight hundred young people who came out to cheer us on. The acceptance I felt from the audience was overwhelming, and really gratifying.

The golden throats of the capacity crowd were united in cheers.

The El Rey show ended, we went backstage, and the crowd continued to cheer for thirty minutes. Unfortunately, we had run through all our songs. There were no more on the album, and Joe Jackson had vanished in a green mist, but I wanted to give the crowd more.

So we went out and did "Lucy in the Sky with Diamonds"— the Shatner way!

Sure, my groovy premise for *The Transformed Man* had long been forgotten, but in the forty intervening years, I was the one who transformed. The audience transformed. The people in front of me at the El Rey *got it*.

I. Was. Vindicated.

I'm not a vulgar man, but at the end of the number, I raised my middle finger into the air. I raised it high, I raised it proud. It wasn't so much a "fuck you," but a more rock-and-roll version of "I'm number one!"

The spotlight caught it and held it. It was power, it was defiance, and it was . . .

Transformative.

And I held it up high enough for Freddy de Cordova to see in Heaven.

Shatner Gets Serious

My musical career is one of the best examples of the mighty power of saying "yes." I said "yes" to doing a trippy, experimental album in 1968. I was certainly flogged aplenty for it, but a few years later, a young man said "yes" to buying it, enjoyed it, and asked me to further explore my musical horizons. Ben and I later said "yes" to performing in a series of Priceline commercials, which were seen by David E. Kelley, who was inspired to cast me as Denny Crane in *The Practice*, which then led to *Boston Legal*, which then led to two Emmy awards. There have been a few sour notes along the way, but the praises of "yes" are certainly worth singing.

Or at least speak-singing.

SECOND RULE FOR TURNING 80:
Don't Be Afraid to Ask for Help

WANTED: ONE SPOTTER NEEDED FOR WELL-KNOWN MEDIA PERSONALITY

ARE YOU A MOTIVATED SELF-STARTER, WITH A GOOD EYE FOR DETAIL? AND CRUMBS? Then you have what it takes to work for an actor-writer-director-philanthropist-horseman-singer-songwriter who has just entered his eightieth year.

Duties: Spotting. Not in the lifting weights way, but in the "Sir, I spotted a stain on the front of your shirt; here's a napkin" way. Your employer has noticed certain maladies associated with octogenarianism, most notably drippings.

This job demands that the applicant keep an eye out for the telltale drippings, crumbs, and spots that sometimes appear on the shirts of those of an advanced age. You will be asked to be on the lookout for such things 24/7, as your employer has reached an age where he is no longer able to notice, yet wants to give the illusion that he does.

Position responsibilities also include monitoring the corners of employer's mouth for crumbs, the interior of employer's nostrils for mucous (wet *and* dry), and employer's ear canals for buildup of wax and hair, and mitigating other telltale signs of age. Strong interpersonal skills are needed to discreetly inform employer about such things without drawing attention to them. Especially before he goes on camera to tape his hit talk show on the Biography Channel, *Raw Nerve*.

Other duties include monitoring length of time employer's car signal is on after vehicle turn has been completed, observing eyes for crust, and shushing.

Shushing skills will most likely be called upon for theatrical events, where employer has been suffering age-induced loss of indoor voice. Employer was recently at an equestrian show with grandkids that featured a film of a horse being born. Pair of eighty-year-old ears meant employer was unable to carefully monitor his volume while using such explanatory phrases as "afterbirth" and "horse vagina" to his young guests. You will be asked to shush him before strangers do— strangers who will then blog/tweet about it in an embarrassing manner.

Do you have what it takes to help a man show the world that he still has what it takes? Then apply today. In person, with a cover letter. (Employer not too good with the whole computer thing.)

Must be good with children, horses, science fiction fans, and William Shatner.

CHAPTER 16

RULE: Don't Trust the Facebook

M y mouth hung open in shock, my shocked pupils scanning the computer screen for any sign . . . of me.

But there was nothing. My identity was gone. Or at least my modern identity was gone. Erased. Forgotten. My Face had been removed from the Book!

I am, of course, talking about the Facebook.

FUN FACTNER: Young people often lose the "the" in front of "the Facebook." They don't usually properly add it until they hit sixty or so. With age comes wisdom! And perfect grammar!

I had had my Facebook profile for a few years. I'd been taking quizzes, tending to my Farmville animals, poking and getting poked, and in March of 2011, the overlords inside the fortress at Facebook mountain decided that I was a fake William Shatner and deleted me.

Deleted!

Do you know what that feels like, in this modern age? To be deemed a fake? And then entirely erased?

I've been called a fake a few times, but no one *ever* had the powers of deletion over my entire personality. I was an unwitting hero in a Philip K. Dick novel. (ATTENTION HOLLYWOOD PRODUCERS HOLDING THE RIGHTS TO VARIOUS PHILIP K. DICK PROPERTIES: I am available if the price is right. We can talk script later.)

California had recently passed a law making it illegal to impersonate someone on Facebook, and it seemed as though the social networking site had decided to play it safe and delete the most popular William Shatner of all from Facebook. Keep in mind I would happily see the arrest of anyone faking me, and one day hope to glory in the sight of a mug shot labeled POLLAK, KEVIN.

I didn't realize it at the time, but there is more than one William Shatner on Facebook. How can you tell us apart? Well, the real William Shatner does not want you to click on that hilarious cat video, nor do I want to meet you in a mall parking lot to "just hang and see what happens." Although I will meet you in a mall parking lot to watch a hilarious cat video. But it had better be hilarious—my time is precious. How precious? I'm the real William Shatner! The real William Shatner is busy!

I didn't know what to do. I couldn't log on to Facebook, because I no longer existed in their eyes.

Then it hit me—*Paul!* Paul would solve everything!

I needed to contact my web guru, Paul Camuso. He runs my website, set up my Facebook account, helps me when the computing machine on my desk is doing that beeping thing. Perhaps he could help reinstate the virtual William Shatner and get me back to the important business of poking my friend, the virtual Adrian Zmed.

Paul, as usual, had some sage advice: Take the issue public. Virtually.

"But how?" I demanded. "I no longer have an account. I'm no longer me!"

He reminded me of the other virtual Shatner he had created for me. I harkened back to a conversation with a lovely actress not so long ago . . .

> RULE: If You're Going to Keep Working in Flashbacks in Your Latest Writing Project, Come up with a Catchy Flashback Branding Device

WILLIAMFLASHBACKNER

"The Twittah?" I asked. "What's that?"

"You know, 'Twittah.' Everyone's awn it. A-ha-ha-ha-ha-hawh!"

I should perhaps explain that the person I was talking to was the lovely Fran Drescher, and in her Queens accent she was trying to "hip" me to the latest technological craze. I have only one of my original hips left, so I look for any help I can in that area.

She was a big fan of this "Twittah," said it was a good way to reach out to fans, and asked if I was on it.

I looked around the set of *Raw Nerve* to the handful of people on Team Shatner and asked, "Am I on the Twittah?"

I was not, but soon I was, and before long, @WilliamShatner on Twitter had more than six hundred thousand followers. And I owe it all to . . . well, Paul Camuso.

To many, I will always be the quintessential twenty-third-century man, but when it comes to technology—in many respects—I am hopelessly mired in the twentieth century. The first part of the twentieth century. The part without all the buttons and Delete keys.

Don't get me wrong, I *understand* technology, but often I can't *do* technology. I get the mechanics, but I'm not that mechanical. I mean, I understand how to change a tire, but I usually call AAA when a tire needs to be changed.

Of course, I'm not a *total* Luddite. After all I'm writing this book on a computer and

[SEGMENT OF MEMOIR MISSING]

RULE: Hit "Save" Every Few Minutes, or You Will Lose Giant Portions of Your *Shatner Rules* Manuscript

Fine—I'm a Luddite. I know how to turn on a computer, but the turning off part leaves me flummoxed. And I cannot leave something on when I leave a room. My father was always running around, turning off lights, and so do I. But turning off a computer is more than a money-saving act; it is a rebellion against society. You are turning your back on a conduit to modern communication; you are ignoring the drumbeat of today's society! You don't just unplug; you disconnect. Turning *off* a computer is turning *on* rebellion!

FUN FACTNER: When William Shatner gets going about technology, he sometimes has trouble sticking to Twitter's 140-character limit.

I've been keeping it a secret for years, especially from the good people in advertising who employ me on occasion. In fact, if you visit YouTube (hopefully someone will show me how to do that soon), you can see me singing the praises of the Commodore VIC-20, "the wonder computer of the eighties," promising "great games" and opportunities for "the whole family to learn computing." All for the bargain price of "under three hundred dollars." (You can get one of these VIC-20s on eBay for about ninety bucks now. Apparently, the wonders of this wonder computer ceased pretty quickly.)

In 1976, Bell Labs hired me to host a short industrial film called *Microworld*, in which I explained the wonders of the microprocessor—"the brain of the modern electronic system"— the silicon chip, solid-state technology! Again, this film—and my giant, broad jacket lapels—can be viewed on YouTube, a by-product of such technology.

Fortunately, I have the help that I need. One of my assistants was good enough to set up my Twitter account for me, and on June 24, 2008, I tweeted, "Learning about this fascinating site." Okay, it's no "Watson, come quick, I need you," but it was a very important first foray for me in this very important communication medium. This is a great way for me to interact with fans, and much more enjoyable than dropping the f-bomb when someone gives me a "Beam me up, Scotty."

Since that humble tweetinning, I have used Twitter to keep fans abreast of my talk show appearances and charity work, and link them up to my other social networking forays at William Shatner.com and on Facebook (which eventually got undeleted; more on that later). And all my tweets end with "My best, Bill."

Or at least that's how I wanted all of them to end. I sometimes shout my tweets to my assistant, Kathleen, who occasionally shouts back, "Too long!" The courtesy of "my best, Bill" was rudely taking up too much space, so it was shortened to my current sign-off of MBB.

FUN FACTNER: William Shatner sometimes uses a voice-activated recorder to transcribe his tweets. Unfortunately, most voice-activation systems shut off during dramatic pauses.

MBB has become a guessing game for people late to my Twitter game. Folks in the Twitterverse sometimes wonder what it means. I have often considered mixing up my sign-offs, just to keep people guessing.

WILLIAM SHATNER'S ALTERNATE TWITTER SIGN-OFFS

TO!B = Tweet out! Bill
BTUS = Beam *this* up, Scotty!
IYNMIBOMH = If you need me, I'll be on my horse
LTEBGT = Love to everyone but George Takei
W$#*!MDSOICU = Watch *$#*! My Dad Says* or I'll cut you

Oh yes, did I mention *$#*! My Dad Says*? Thirty years ago, I was on the cutting edge of the "wonder computer of the eighties," and then I was on the first television show spun off from a Twitter feed. Justin Halpern, along with masterful comedy duo and *Will &*

Grace creators David Kohan and Max Mutchnick, managed to turn 140 characters about Halpern's cranky old father into a television show, and they asked me to star in it.

FUN FACTNER: Many call the casting of William Shatner as an outspoken, opinionated old man "inspired." Shatner's children call it "typecasting."

I had never heard of the $#*! My Dad Says Twitter feed, and was barely able to figure out my own Twitter feed, and suddenly 10 million

Bill says some shit on the set of *$h*! My Dad Says* in 2011.

people a week were watching the show to see me as Dr. Edison "Ed" Milford Goodson III, a sharp-tongued, politically incorrect man who has his grown son move back home with him. It even won Favorite New TV Comedy at the People's Choice Awards. That didn't stop CBS from canceling it, unfortunately.

Executives don't know $#*!

No matter how much at sea I am with technology, technology always throws its virtual arms around me. My relationship with technology is similar to Michael Corleone's relationship with the Mob: Just when I think I'm out—they pull me back in! And Twitter keeps pulling me in to late night comedy!

Some of you may remember my now famous late night television appearances on *The Tonight Show with Conan O'Brien*, reading the tweets of former vice presidential candidate Sarah Palin. When the fractured nature of the 140-character feed met the somewhat fractured musings of the Grizzly Momma, it occurred to Conan that they felt like poetry. Spoken-word Beat poetry.

Take one Twitter feed, add one stand-up bass, one set of bongos (or is that two bongo?), and one William Shatner, and you have yourself some late night gold.

Conan introduced me to the screaming crowd. I took my spot on a stool and read Sarah's tweets—stone-faced, dry as a bone—while the cool jazz combo played behind me and Conan snapped his fingers.

From sea life, near lush wet rain forests
To energy, housed under frozen tundra, atop permafrost
God most creatively displays his diversity in Alaska.

Tourists from across America, here, loving their forty-
ninth state
I'm reminded one heart, one hope, one destiny, one flag
From sea to . . . sea."

Awesome Alaska night
Sensing summer already winding down.
With fireweed near full bloom
Finally sitting down to pen
Listening to Big & Rich.

Somewhere, the ghost of Johnny Carson was mouthing, "What . . . the . . . fuck?"

We were a hit. Here I was, a technophobe, making poetry and music from technology I could barely comprehend. I was so successful, in fact, that I found myself in Sarah Palin's crosshairs. Her comedic crosshairs, mind you. Thankfully, not the "kill wolves from a helicopter" crosshairs.

While I was making a return appearance on Conan, this time to read from her autobiography, *Going Rogue*, Palin walked onto the stage, grasping a copy of my autobiography *Up Till Now* under her arm. The jazz combo backed her as she read some portions of my book. She got her laughs, all right, and I had to stand there and take it!

Needless to say, Sarah Palin is no William Shatner when it comes to droll Beat poetry. I say to her: Keep your day job! Whatever that is!

Which brings me back to my Facebook crisis. There was no longer a me to protest me getting shut down. And I was getting nowhere online.

Facebook gave me a telephone number, but all I got was a recording telling me to log on to Facebook, which I could no longer do. Eventually, when we did contact a human—via phone, not poking—I was told that they would need a scanned "government-issued ID" from me.

Would you send a scanned driver's license or birth certificate to a stranger at Facebook? Would you do it if there were a chance that some clown could take it and put it on a T-shirt and then toss it up on eBay? No way. I mean, you can buy my kidney stones, but no one may steal my identity.

It seemed as though I was never going to get back on the Facebook. But then, sage Paul, from his den of tubes, wires, and little motors that go *whhhrrrrrr*, reminded me that there was still Twitter. We decided to use social media to fix social media! I grabbed my voice-activated whatchamacallit, and tweeted: "Facebook disabled my acct. this weekend as an imposter acct. Now they want me to prove that it's me. Don't they know who I am? MBB."

That is all it took.

Within thirty minutes, my good, virtual name had been restored. I once more had an account on the Facebook! Again, I could take part in the community that has revolutionized the way we communicate with one another. William Shatner would not be denied.

Although frankly, I wish Adrian Zmed would knock it off with all the poking. I mean, I know I started it, but it has to end somewhere, Adrian!

WILLIAM SHATNER ANSWERS YOUR FACEBOOK QUESTIONS

In addition to my on-again, off-again Facebook profile, I also have an official fan page on the site where people sometimes post questions to my wall. I would like to take this opportunity to answer some of those questions. These are all *real* questions.

Brenna Casper

Do u know where Leonard went??? He hasn't been on Facebook for a long time!! :)

I don't know. But you're using the wrong emoticon for discussing a Vulcan. The correct one is :| . Remember—no smiling! (But, like most people, Leonard probably has ditched Facebook and spends all his time on Twitter.)

Joan Arnet

When do you come to Switzerland? :-)

When I get the e-mail alert PRICELINE DEALS—DON'T SWISS OUT ON SAVINGS!

James Lopez

Hi Mr. Shatner,

You were in Pittsburgh, PA in the 1970s and stayed with my dad's brother and his wife. They are Joe and Betty Lopez and had a large pool and a horse. My dad John and mom Kathy were there also. Just wondered if you recall that stay back then.

Okay, buddy, I know what you're getting at. I'll return the bath towels! I accidentally packed them. Also, sorry about the wet horse. You shouldn't keep those things so close to the pool.

Michael Deforest

In Australia, does the water *really* flush down the other way, Bill?

I don't know. I never flush. That's what my spotter is for (see my ad on Craigslist).

Fredrick Aman

Happy birthday, Bill! You're the greatest Canadian actor ever! ;)

Okay, that's not a question. But I felt it should be shared.

Allison Byrne

Hey, Bill! We still on for dinner next week?

Let me know if you're buying.

Adam Lars

Happy birthday, you old condom-stretcher.

I told you, I've only ever gotten money for performing. That is obviously a skilled trade.

Wendy McDonald

Bill—I fell in love with you when I was 9 years old. I will be 55 this year. How's that for fandom!!!

Your fandom is beyond reproach, but I do find some fault with your depressing mathematical calculations.

Nila Martinez

SUP KIRK? NICE TO HAVE BEEN ABLE TO GROW UP WITH YOU BRAH YOU DA BOMB..ALOHA..

I am fluent in French and English. Neither is helping me here.

Sarah Goldfarb

I'm so glad you are Jewish!!!!! Want to come to my house for Passover?

Certainly. But only if I get to ask *all* four questions. I only travel if it's a starring role.

CHAPTER 17

RULE: Remember Where You Came from . . . Eh?

Every celebrity bio needs a bombshell. Be it addiction, abuse, shocking sexual conquest. I promised the publisher of *Shatner Rules* a big one. So here it is. Get ready. I am about to drop the bombshell . . .

I am a Canadian.

FUN FACTNER: Actor William Shatner is Canadian!

I'll let that sink in. And for my American readers, I'll let you all take a break from reading this book so that you can go Google "Canadian" and figure out what one is. Here's a hint: We are the people who live up north who aren't Alaskan and who aren't Santa.

In fact, I'm so Canadian that I'm not even an American. Seriously. I can't vote here. I can't vote in Canada either, which is why politicians on both sides of the border never worry about the Shatner vote. Although I have a green card, which means some American politicians would work very hard to try to deport me. I kept this a secret from Sarah Palin when I met her on *The Tonight Show with Conan O'Brien.*

To stay in this great nation of America, I must prove that I can do a job that cannot be held by an American. I do the job of being William Shatner. No one else can do it. Kevin Pollak tries with that "impression" of his, and if he continues to do so, I'll see . . . about . . . having . . . him . . . deported.

(NOTE: This rule only applies to Kevin Pollak.)

You know who knows I'm Canadian? Other Canadians. I am a celebrated figure north of the border. In as much as Canadians ever "celebrate" things. And when Canada hosted the 2010 Olympics in Vancouver, I was invited to participate in the closing ceremonies. How could I refuse? Canadians would have been furious. Although they wouldn't have expressed their fury.

Seriously, the only way to get a rise out of a Canadian? Place him on a hydraulic lift.

Actually, Canadians and hydraulics don't really mix, as evidenced by the Olympic ceremonies. They outfitted the BC Place Stadium with a false floor, about twelve feet above the normal floor, on which the action would take place. And during the opening ceremonies, four mighty steel pillars were to rise up from this floor. Four torchbearers were to simultaneously walk up to these pillars, touch their torches to the base of them, and then a river of fire would travel up the metal to light the cauldron that held the Olympic flame. A spectacular sight for a spectacular event! One that would be watched by billions!

The four Maple Leaf Olympians selected for this task would be hockey hero Wayne Gretzky, speed skater Catriona Le May Doan, skier Nancy Greene, and basketball all star Steve Nash. What an honor, what a thrill!

What a blunder.

After many rehearsals and test runs, on opening night, the fourth pillar wouldn't rise. Nothing. Each athlete stood there waiting, billions of people around the world watching them slowly getting coated in their own flop sweat. The event director shouted into their earpieces, "Hold it! Hold it! Hold it! It's gonna come up. Wait! Wait! Wait!"

Nothing doing. Eventually, three of the four walked up to their pillars to light the torch, while poor Catriona Le May Doan stood there awkwardly, wishing she could speed skate as far away as possible.

That evening, Canada medaled in embarrassment. But at least I knew they would definitely iron out the kinks before the closing ceremonies. Right?

Right?

If anything, the closing ceremonies were to be bigger and more spectacular than the opening ceremonies. It would be a supreme celebration of all things Canadian! Taking the stage that evening would be me, Michael J. Fox, Catherine O'Hara, and a dizzying display of giant inflatable moose, dancing Mounties, lumberjacks in canoes, a small child dressed as a hockey puck, and inflatable beavers (normally only found in some of Vancouver's seedier "marital aid" stores). The spectacular promised to be the least understated thing in Canadian history.

There would also be a huge concert of Canada's biggest rockers, like Alanis Morissette, Nickelback, Avril Lavigne, and many more I've never heard of.

Canada also wanted to show the world that it had a sense of humor about the opening ceremony debacle. The closing ceremony started with a mime named Yves Dagenais, who rose up on a platform, plugged some extension cords together, and then mimed pulling up the faulty fourth pillar from the floor. It rose spectacularly, and Catriona Le May Doan emerged and finally got to light her torch.

The crowd positively roared. In fact, it may have been the warmest reception a mime has ever gotten!

The closing ceremonies went along without a hitch as I headed to the basement area, to my assigned hydraulic platform, which would carry me to the floor so I could deliver an inspiring and comedic monologue. We had done a few physical run-throughs, but we hadn't run my lines.

That's not a problem for me; I tend to memorize things quickly, but thankfully my old friend the teleprompter would be at my feet. If I blanked momentarily, thanks to the teleprompter, the sixty thousand people in the stadium, and billions around the world, would not see me coated in my own flop sweat.

So I'm in this basement, this subterranean cavern of hydraulic machinery, sound and light equipment, fiber-optic cables, and lots of people running around in headsets looking like they know what they're doing. I can feel the sheer excitement, the energy, of the event going on above me. In my earpiece, I can hear the director calmly giving his instructions to the crew. Fellow Canadian Neil Young was performing on my platform as I readied my entrance.

Neil finishes, huge cheers. His platform lowers, and there he is in front of me, guitar over his neck, resplendent in muttonchop sideburns.

"Hello, Bill," he says.

"Hello, Neil," say I. And he heads off into the night.

FUN FACTNER: Every Canadian knows each other and is on a first name basis. (Hi, Celine! Hope you're enjoying the book!)

Two technicians run over to my platform as I go over my lines in my head. They both furtively attend to my teleprompter, which . . . is . . . not . . . working.

As with the mighty steel arm that never rose, my teleprompter worked fine in the rehearsals. Now it was on the fritz. My earpiece, which was working quite well, helped me hear the director say, "Sixty seconds to Shatner!"

Never mind flop sweating on stage—I was doing it quite well in this subterranean studio. I knew my lines, but . . . what if I didn't know my lines?! Christina Aguilera has performed the national anthem more times than she's had hot meals! And she flubbed it at the 2011 Super Bowl. It's not a long song, and she should know it, but she blanked in front of a huge audience. An Olympic-sized audience. The same size that I was about to face.

"Put Shatner on the platform!" said the voice in my earpiece. Again, the earpiece was working splendidly, unlike my teleprompter.

The workmen now skillfully started repairing the platform by pounding it with a hammer. The teleprompter was working when Neil Young went up, apparently. What the hell did Neil do? Did his heavy sideburns burn out the hydraulics and cause an electrical malfunction?

"Shatner on the platform, *now!*"

A production assistant shuffled me onto the platform, gripping my arm. A good hangman can supposedly guess the condemned's weight just by shaking his hand. That's how I felt! I was being led to my doom. Except that the platform would rise up instead of drop.

I was literally being pushed. I began to think of fellow Canadian Robert Goulet. He forgot the words to the national anthem at a Muhammad Ali/Sonny Liston prizefight in 1965. They never forgave him. Poor Robert! (We were on a first name basis, you see . . .)

The platform began to rise, the mic in my hand trembled, one of the technicians gave one last swing to the hammer and—

The teleprompter fluttered on. I began to rise.

The lights, the sound, the energy of what I witnessed when I rose up through the floor was unlike anything I have ever experienced. I once did the coin toss at the Rose Bowl, and the cheers hit you like a shockwave. Your body trembles as it passes through you. But at least I was no longer shaking from fear.

This is what I said. As you're reading, scream your head off at the end of every line, to make yourself feel like you were in the audience.

> **My name is Bill, and I am proud to be a Canadian.**
>
> **My pride is an immense as this majestic country who hosted these 2010 games.**
>
> **As a Canadian, I am proud of many things.**
>
> **Our magnificent lakes. Our stunning sunsets.**
>
> **Proud of my hometown, Montreal.**
>
> **Proud of the University at McGill and the words "*Je Suis Canadien.*"**

(NOTE: I made sure to make this sound as French as possible. We Canadians love doing that!)

And the fact that we are a people who know how to make love in a canoe.

And our health care system covers the splinters.

I'm proud of our Rocky Mountains, our glaciers, our loons!

(NOTE: If you say "loon" in front of sixty thousand Canadians, sixty thousand Canadians will then impersonate the loon's call. They love doing that, too.)

And that, to Canadians, minus thirty degrees is just another sign of global warming.

It's a big country. We dream big, you have to, in a land that is the Final Frontier.

(NOTE: When making a speech to a billion people, it's best not to go too esoteric with the references.)

And, damnit, I'm proud of the fact that Canadians, after four beers, in front of worldwide television, can successfully pronounce "the Strait of Juan de Fuca" without being censored.

FUN FACTNER: The Strait of Juan de Fuca is a one-hundred-mile-long body of water that serves as the principal outlet for the Georgia Strait and Puget Sound, which then empties into Lake Smuttyjoke.

For I am William Shatner, one of 35 million Canadians, and we dream big!

My speech, my love letter to the nation I adore, was a beautiful, big dream. Amid the cheers, my platform lowered. Triumphantly.

I looked down at the teleprompter, the mother's teat ready for my suckle of safety, flickering lightly.

I never needed it.

I was so thrilled, I almost jumped for joy. But . . . I'm Canadian. We don't do that sort of thing.

CHAPTER 18

RULE: If You Look a Gift Horse in the Mouth, You Might Find More Gifts!

C an a negotiation ever go too far? Sometimes. Sometimes, you can push too far and drive the deal off a cliff.

But, if you manage to stop just short of driving off a cliff, you'll have a pretty nice view. Or at least really good seats to a very important event.

Performing at the closing ceremony of the Vancouver Olympics certainly had its perks. Team Shatner runs thirteen deep—me, my wife Elizabeth, my three beloved daughters, my three beloved sons-in-law, and my assorted and beloved grandkids. The organizers of the ceremony were good enough to fly all of us up to enjoy the event. It was a real celebration of family togetherness, and one I will cherish forever.

The scenery in Vancouver is amazing, especially if you also have a great view of the people you love.

Seriously, you can't put a price on such things. So let's talk freebies!

We were offered hockey tickets—rinkside! To watch the United States take on Canada. It was *the* hottest ticket of the entire Olympics. No one is crazier about hockey than Canadians. It's the one place where we can be aggressive without shame or guilt or fear of being too showy.

This was a matchup against America! Our neighbors to the south, who don't know we exist. What better way to get the attention of Americans than to beat their team at hockey!

> **RULE: If You Are a Canadian and Want America's Attention—Beat Them at Hockey. Or, If You Can't Do That, Offer Them a Canadian Beer. Our Beer Is Good. Americans Like Beer.**

What a thrill. What an honor. What a conundrum for me.

They were offering four tickets. There are thirteen of us, more than a few of whom are rabid hockey fans.

As the patriarch of the clan, and the man whose face would be needed to gain entry to the event, I had to reserve one ticket for myself. Elizabeth, being my wife, is traditionally my plus one, so she would be going, too. Doling out the others would be a bit of a challenge.

We were all gathered at a dinner table in a restaurant. I explained that I had these free tickets, and I could see my sons-in-law Joel and Andrew sit bolt upright with anticipation. The two of them are huge hockey fans. I know they're hockey fans, they know I know they're hockey fans. Who else could I possibly take along for this historic sporting event?

"I thought I would take along Joel and Andrew, since they are such huge fans. They are the biggest hockey fans in the family, correct?"

Everyone nodded, and Joel and Andrew did everything in their power not to stand up, high-five one another, and shout *"In your face!"* at their respective wives and children. But they conducted themselves with quiet dignity and grace.

I had begun to dig in to dinner when my daughter Leslie piped up and said, "You know, Dad, Eric and Grant really like hockey."

Eric and Grant are two of my teenaged grandkids, who were both eagerly wolfing down their dinners. Joel and Andrew swallowed hard and stared at their plates, drumming their fingers nervously.

"Oh, really?" I said. "I didn't know that. Well . . ."

It was time to negotiate. My first move?

I excused myself.

RULE: When You Need to Stall, Hit the Stall

I went to the restroom, and paced back and forth. Joel and Andrew love hockey more than anything! Eric and Grant? Well, they liked hockey okay, but did they like it as much as Joel and Andrew?

Probably not. For one thing, Joel and Andrew had about fifty years' worth of fandom between them over my grandkids. Eric and Grant needed a few more years to develop their own typically unhealthy adult relationship with the sport.

I splashed some water on my face and looked in the mirror. What was the negotiation endgame? Would I be a bad dad to my sons-in-law, or a bad grandpa to Eric and Grant? I needed a solution.

I returned to the table and tucked my napkin under my chin, armed with the weapon that solves everything.

Bribery.

"Eric, Grant, instead of going to the hockey game, what do you say I put a little money in your accounts? The value of the tickets, maybe?"

If my daughter's eyes had made a sound when they rolled, I would have been knocked over by the sonic shockwave. Leslie was used to this—all my daughters are used to this. Dinner with Dad rarely went without a debate or negotiation of some sort.

Negotiation aids the digestion! It warms you up for the eventual argument with the waiter over the check.

My grandsons pondered this monetary offer between them for a second.

"Nah," said Eric. "We'll take the tickets."

Grant agreed, in between mouthfuls. These grandkids of mine were tough negotiators. I was proud. They retained a unified front, wouldn't negotiate without the other, stayed strong, showed that it wasn't about money, it was about principle. And about watching grown men punch each other in the head on ice skates.

They got the tickets.

The grandkids won. It would be me, Elizabeth, and the two boys rinkside. It was then that I realized that good negotiating skills might not only be in the genetics of my blood relatives, because Joel played the ultimate trump card in any back and forth negotiation.

His eyes filled with tears.

Bravo, I thought to myself, while taking a big swig of sparkling water. Well played, young Joel! Crying always works!

FUN FACTNER: William Shatner's son-in-law Joel Gretsch is a busy actor on both the small and big screens. And like all good actors, he can cry on cue.

I was very impressed, and waited to see which one of his nephews, seeing his uncle tear up, would be the first to fold and hand over a ticket. My other son-in-law, Andrew, is a special-effects artist. If he could have, he would have run away from the restaurant to fashion some sort of crying apparatus from latex and wire, but Joel beat him to the moist, sobby punch.

But neither boy noticed. Elizabeth did.

"Joel," she said with great empathy, "you can have my ticket."

Lovely Elizabeth. She stood by her man by agreeing not to sit with him.

There was much celebration as Joel danced on the table, and much relief for me. My wonderful Elizabeth had taken the heat off me. I was a great grandpa and a great father-in-law. And I was proud of my brood of negotiators.

(NOTE: Later I found out that the tickets were going for $40,000 a pop on the street. Those little grandkids of mine were kicking themselves. They lost eighty grand! **The Negotiator had triumphed!***)*

Until the next day, when I got a call on the phone from one of the Olympic organizers.

"Sorry, Mr. Shatner," he quavered, "I don't know how to tell you this, but your four tickets are gone."

"What?!?" I yelled. "You *have* to be joking."

"I wish I were, sir," he apologized. "We think someone stole them. Did you know they were going for forty grand a pop? That's $41,939 American."

They had lost my tickets. My $160,000 ($167,756 American) worth of hockey enjoyment. And family togetherness, and family harmony.

There is one negotiation tool that should be used sparingly, only in case of an emergency. This was an emergency. I had to take a metaphorical hammer, smash some symbolic glass, and pull a real diva fit. Or, since I'm male, a divo fit.

FUN FACTNER: In Canada, even diva fits are punctuated with "pleases," "thank yous," and "whatever is okays."

"You promised me, I'm here, I'm your star, you're shafting me. *I won't go on!!!*"

I hung up the phone, the foul stench of my bluff hanging in the air. There was no way in heck I would bail on my native land over a few hockey tickets. But in a tough negotiation, you must be willing to at least *sound* tough.

The Olympic official called back a few hours later. "Mr. Shatner, I got three tickets."

Was this good enough? Maybe. Joel and the grandsons could go. I'd be the best father-in-law, and best grandfather. I could win a gold medal in patriarchal love!

I was about to say yes when the Evil Negotiator appeared. I could feel my sinister Vandyke beard growing on my face. Three tickets were not enough. The original four were not enough. I had to bring the hammer down!

"*I need six tickets!*" I yelled, "I'll take the three, but . . . *I need six tickets.* You *must* make this happen."

I almost said "please," but then remembered my evil facial hair. Two hundred forty thousand dollars' worth of tickets. To watch a hockey game.

Would the full-on eruption of Mount Shatner be enough to close this deal?

Joel and Andrew, Eric and Grant, and Elizabeth and I loved the hockey game. So did the man seated next to us, who was weeping and biting on his Canadian flag when our team won in overtime against the USA. I had perhaps forever made an enemy of a Canadian Olympic official—and if he is reading this, I apologize—but I had negotiated myself the title of World's Greatest Dad/Granddad/Husband/Hockey Fan.

Am I proud of what I did? I'm prouder of other things I've done. But I do wish I had held out for more money with the whole kidney stones thing.

By the way, at the eleventh hour, my grandkids tried to see if there was any possibility of revisiting my "money in their bank accounts" offer instead of the tickets.

Let me tell you—those two will not soon forget the day they first encountered the Evil Negotiator.

CHAPTER 19

RULE: Know Which Conversations Require a Bullet-Proof Vest

"The greatest love in my life was my first squirrel."

Did I say this? No, although I have formed very strong bonds with several horses, many Dobermans, and the occasional orca.

Is this the title of some self-help book, à la *Everything I Needed to Know I Learned in Kindergarten*? Nope. This above statement was made on the set of my television show *Aftermath*, by one Mr. Bernhard Goetz.

The greatest love of his life was a squirrel.

With this statement, I learned that New York City's "Subway Vigilante" had turned into New York's foremost squirrel enthusiast. He lives with several of the creatures in his small apartment, and he has the scratches up and down his arms to prove it.

I imagine squirrels are the only one of God's creatures who are perfectly comfortable asking Bernhard Goetz for five dollars.

Bill and Bernhard Goetz discuss squirrels and guns on *Aftermath* in 2010.

Aftermath is a show I host and executive produce for the Biography Channel, the same channel that airs my other talk show, *Raw Nerve*, which I also executive produce.

(This means there's another 22.5 hours of daily programming on Bio that I need to start filling. Thank goodness I'm a multitasker. For instance, I am typing this while on the set of *Aftermath*. Mary Kay Letourneau and her husband, Vili Fualaau, are staring at me. Might need to pick this chapter up later.)

Okay, it's later. Had a very nice conversation with the Fualaaus. Check your local listings.

Aftermath is an hour-long program that takes an in-depth look at what happens to people who are yanked from their anonymous, everyday lives and then dropped down hard onto the front pages of newspapers and tabloids. I sit down with these people, some forgotten, some not, and discuss with them how their lives have changed since their fifteen minutes of fame, or infamy.

It is an amazing experience for me—professionally and personally. In my years on Earth, I have met presidents, the occasional religious leader, a spare royal or two. And in 2010, I found myself sitting within two feet of a man most famous for shooting four teenagers he thought were out to rob him.

Goetz's life has certainly changed since that day on a crowded subway train in 1984. He's no longer the cause célèbre of the citizens of a dangerous and crime-ridden New York. He's not front-page news anymore. He buys and sells electronics on the Internet, and flies below the radar financially, so to speak, because of the massive civil judgment brought upon him by his brain-damaged victim, Darrell Cabey. But he's still pretty quick with a gun.

How do I know this? He pulled one on me.

Halfway through our interview, Goetz was explaining how—after a brutal mugging in the early 1980s—he got hold of an illegal handgun and started practicing his quick draw. He would practice with the loaded weapon in his home, in his office, even in the elevators of his apartment building.

I imagine many of his neighbors—when the doors of the elevators would open revealing an armed Bernhard Goetz—would stay put and say, "I'll wait for the next one."

It was during the course of this discussion that one of my producers got the idea to give Goetz a gun and let him show me his quick-draw technique. While the producer hid somewhere behind the cameras, I imagine.

We made certain the gun was empty, and after many, many hours of checking and rechecking the gun, Goetz made me stand up, not three feet away, and demonstrate what he did on the subway that day.

Quick draw. Bang. Quick draw. Bang. Bang and bang.

It's a strange thing to stare into the eyes of such a figure, one who really hasn't aged much since his time in the spotlight, and have him draw a gun on you and pull the trigger. And he's a man who has no remorse about what he did.

And he kept doing it, whipping it out of his waistband, pulling the trigger, aiming the gun at me, the cameramen, people standing around. It was almost childlike. I said to him, "People kid around with pistols like that, do that fast draw, like we did as kids. But you fast drew, and actually fired a bullet."

"Yeah . . . so?"

And that "so" is the difference between people like Bernie Goetz and you and me. (I'll assume you're a pretty together person based on the wisdom of your *Shatner Rules* purchase.)

That's not much of a difference when you get right down to it. But Bernhard Goetz was, and is, living in his truth. And the truth is amorphous; it is what it is to the person who is living it. And with *Aftermath*, I want people to share their truth, unfiltered, without judgment. I am a man of some opinions, but I keep them to myself on *Aftermath*.

That being said . . . after the taping, another producer came up to me and asked if I was scared of Goetz. I said, "No." He said, "Well, you looked scared." And I replied, "Well, I've never been that close to anyone that crazy before."

Keep in mind, I've signed autographs at hundreds of science fiction conventions.

Aftermath has allowed me to meet fascinating characters: the aforementioned Fualaaus came on to discuss their scandalous May-September (of the following year) romance; I spoke to survivors of the 1992 anti-government standoff at Ruby Ridge; I also chatted with New York's notorious society girl–turned–Mayflower Madam Sydney Biddle Barrows; Iraq War hostage Jessica Lynch; and Unabomber brother Dave Kaczynski.

I even did a prison interview with Lee Boyd Malvo, the teenager who—along with John Allen Muhammad—murdered at least ten people in 2002 in the DC Sniper spree.

At the end of our conversation, I asked him, "Will God forgive you?"

He said, "If I can forgive myself."

Was I talking to a murderer? Yes, but mostly I was also talking to a young guy who was horribly manipulated by a man he trusted and is now serving a life sentence. He has written letters to many of the survivors, and to the families of the murdered, apologizing for his actions.

That interview with the sniper took weeks to happen. I would sit in my office between 4 and 6 P.M. every day, with the entire crew, waiting for the phone to ring. It finally went down when Malvo got access to the prison pay phone.

While *Aftermath* has its share of the infamous, I've also had the opportunity to meet two men I deeply admire: tobacco industry whistleblower Jeffrey Wigand, and Daniel Ellsberg, the former military analyst turned peace activist who released the Pentagon Papers to *The New York Times* in 1971.

Ellsberg copied three thousand top secret pages of analysis and four thousand pages of government documents in forty-seven volumes, all of which showed that the Johnson administration had lied to the public and Congress about the war in Vietnam. It's hard to realize the significance of this action, and the effort that it took, in this era of technological ease, when I can tell half a million people what I had for breakfast in the blink of an eye via Twitter.

FUN FACTNER: William Shatner usually goes with fruit and a protein or grain, along with some vitamin supplements, for breakfast.

Why am I doing *Aftermath*? Well, perhaps it's time for me to sit in the hot seat and discuss my own truth.

My wife Nerine died in 1999, after battling a severe addiction to alcohol, one that both she and I were powerless to control over the course of our marriage. The coroner ruled that she had died of an accidental drowning. She had alcohol and

Valium in her system at the time of death, and I discovered her at the bottom of our pool when I returned from a family dinner in Orange County, California.

Some months later, I went to New York, along with one of my daughters, to be interviewed on a tabloid news show about a television project I was involved in. I sat down across from the woman who was to interview me, and what was the first question out of her mouth?

"What's it feel like to murder your wife?"

Needless to say, she didn't get a follow-up question. I ended the interview and demanded the tape. My daughter started crying, the *reporter* started crying, and I stormed out.

Apparently, when there is an unnatural death of someone at an early age, there's a good chance a family member was involved, and—for the briefest period of time—I was a suspect in Nerine's death. It's standard operating procedure. The husband is *always* the first suspect. But I was cleared within minutes of the police arriving at my home.

I was cleared in the eyes of the law, anyway. In the jaded and jaundiced eyes of the tabloid press? Well, that's a different, under-researched story.

And within days of her death, as I was experiencing a whirl-pool of emotions, grief coming from many different directions all at once, dragging me down, I got a phone call from *The National Enquirer*. They were going to run a story saying that I was the prime suspect in the murder of my wife.

They offered me money to participate in the story, to tell my side. If I didn't play ball, they were going to run with the angle that I was a murderer.

What would you do? Probably the same thing I did.

I gave them my story, took their money, and used every cent of it to fund the Nerine Shatner Friendly House, a center for women recovering from alcohol and substance abuse. It's a home where up to twenty women at a time can get the help they need to fight their addictions.

Did you know that? Maybe you didn't. But you probably heard some of the allegations about my supposed role in her death. That's because in America, you are guilty on page 1, and exonerated on page 30. (Also, many tabloid reporters can't spell "exoneration," so they decide to skip the whole thing entirely.)

And I wanted *Aftermath* to be a show where the exonerated—and the punished—could speak, long after the press had packed up their microphones and moved onto the next scandal. I want to give people a pulpit to tell their side of the story—their truth—after they've been declared guilty by the press and the public.

I know what condemnation in the media feels like, and it is a terrible thing. It follows you like a comet's tail. So I want to use the media as a tool to give some strength back to these people, no matter what their story.

And that's why I'm doing *Aftermath*.

My interview with Mr. Goetz ended, and I began to pack up my things and get ready to go home. He came up to me and asked for a favor. After I was convinced that the gun had been taken away, I agreed.

"Can I get a picture?" he asked, holding his camera phone.

Bernhard Goetz and I took a picture together, and I gave him an autograph. I made it out to him alone. If the squirrel wants one, he can come to the next convention.

CHAPTER 20

RULE: Talk Is Cheap——Unless You Can Make Money with a Talk Show

"**H**ey, Bill," my producer said, rushing into my office. "We got Meat Loaf."

"Oh, all right," I sighed, pulling myself up from my desk. "I'll go easy on the gravy and make sure I spend a little more time on the StairMaster tonight."

"No," she sighed. "Meat Loaf—Meat Loaf as a guest."

"What the hell is a Meat Loaf?"

I really didn't know. I really thought she was talking about food. There appeared to be a very large gap in my pop culture knowledge, one large enough to fit Marvin Lee Aday—the actor and singer who would gain fame as Meat Loaf after selling 43 million copies of his debut album *Bat Out of Hell*.

I was going to interview him for a few hours as a guest on *Raw Nerve*, my talk show on the Biography Channel.

And yes, during the course of our interview, Meat Loaf made me cry.

I've been a guest hundreds of times on as many different talk shows. I've lost count—I see things on YouTube that I don't even remember doing. I've been interviewed by Merv Griffin, Mike Douglas, Alan Thicke, Arsenio Hall, all the ladies on *The View,* all the ladies on *The Talk,* Bill O'Reilly, Oprah, Ellen, Tony Danza, Donny Deutsch, Tom Snyder, Ryan Seacrest, Wayne Brady, Dinah Shore, Graham Norton, Richard and Judy, Crook and Chase, Regis and Kathie Lee, Regis and Kelly, Rosie O'Donnell, Larry King, Howard Stern (many, many times), too many other shock jocks to remember, Henry Rollins, Glenn Beck, Joan Rivers, Jon Stewart, David Brenner, Craig Kilborn, Johnny Carson, the teams at *Good Morning America* and *The Today Show,* Jimmy Kimmel, David Letterman, Jay Leno, Craig Ferguson, and George Lopez, and I've been on Conan O'Brien's shows more times than the Masturbating Bear!

FUN FACTNER: William Shatner's hundreds of talk show appearances over the years have left him with a debilitating case of "couch sores."

So, I've talked myself hoarse over nearly fifty years of talk show appearances. Quite a few of my clips have gone viral, which—nowadays—

is a good thing and doesn't require a shot. I've sung on these shows (most recently Rihanna's "Umbrella" on Conan). I almost lost a William Shatner trivia contest on Kimmel against an uber-fan. I was interviewed by the animated Space Ghost. I was even banned from Carson after a mid-1980s appearance when I talked too much and monopolized our discussion.

It seems some of these talk show hosts prefer to be the ones who get all the laughs.

I've been grilled by guys who are ultra-prepared, reading questions off their little blue cards, and grilled by guys like Stern and Ferguson, who might go in the most outlandish, unexpected directions. I came with stories and things to promote, and I've answered all their questions, but I also observed their questioning.

So I knew one day I would get off that couch and hop behind the desk. The executives at the Biography Channel were interested, and I told them that I wanted to do an interview show with a *Vanity Fair* magazine vibe. I didn't want to do just celebrities; I wanted to interview newsmakers, kings, aristocrats, politicians. I wanted to interview a variety of different kinds of people.

RULE: Advertisers Stop Listening after They Hear the Word "Celebrities"

Okay, so maybe I wouldn't be interviewing newsmakers, kings, aristocrats, and politicians. *Raw Nerve* was going to be a forum for celebrity interviews. But I refused to make it a conventional Q&A where a celebrity hawks his product to a bored audience.

(Not that there's anything wrong with hawking a product, mind you. Have you visited WilliamShatner.com yet? Or have you downloaded *Raw Nerve* episodes from iTunes, as a complement to this chapter?)

First off, this show was going to be called *Raw Nerve*, not *Breakfast with Bill*. (Although that's not off the table. What a wonderful idea for a show! Producers—call me!) Nerves were going to be touched, and they were going to be, well, look at the title. Raw!

Am I a grand inquisitor? Depends on who you talk to. If you talk to any member of my family who has ever shared a meal with me, the answer will be "yes." My daughters have often joked, "It's not dinner with Dad unless someone leaves the table crying." While tears are rare—and they're usually mine (you're not that special, Mr. Loaf)—we do often have spirited discussions at dinner, and I am often the one leading the hard line of questioning.

I'm not a fan of boring conversations. I want to hear something interesting, I want to share something interesting, and I have many methods of getting a rise out of people to help spur discussions. A good debate also burns calories, so you can help yourself to another slice of meat loaf with gravy.

On *Raw Nerve* I try to dig until I find the soul. Sometimes, celebrities get very good at hiding theirs. I want to talk and find out what their "point of entry" was in life, where they truly discovered who they were. I don't what to know what happened to them; I want to know what they felt like when the thing happened. If they are going to plug something, I want them to plug the real human being inside.

A lot of people might ask, "Bill, how can you possibly take on *another* TV project?" Well, *Raw Nerve* is easy—I don't prepare for it.

Nope. I don't do pre-interviews, I don't go over press releases, and I don't sit there and obsess over my little blue cards full of bullet points. I sit down across from the guest, and just start grilling.

(NOTE: If you're ever going to be a guest on Raw Nerve, *clear your calendar and bring a change of clothes.)*

The interview that makes it to air is cut down. Sometimes it takes me several hours to find the raw nerve. I dig, and dig, and dig, and I always find it.

Valerie Bertinelli opened up about sin, adultery, and hell. Ed Asner discussed how his father never forgave him for being born. Weird Al Yankovic explored his feelings about his parents' tragic deaths. Wayne Brady talked about the dissolution of his marriage.

Tim Allen shared with me tales of his alcoholism and stint in prison, Fran Drescher spoke of her rape, Gene Simmons and I discussed Jewish identity, Larry Flynt talked about the assassin's bullet that put him in his wheelchair, Jenna Jameson showed us the ups and downs of porn, and Kelsey Grammer explored the painful family tragedies that have marked his life.

Both Rush Limbaugh and Jon Voight cried!

RULE: A Lot of Conservatives Are Pretty Liberal with the Tears

The hardest nuts to crack? The comedians. Carl Reiner was especially tough. I've known Carl for a long time, and we even acted together on *Boston Legal,* but I could *not* get him to open up about the death of his wife. I've been a widower—I wanted to know if we had shared emotions, feelings. He told some wonderful jokes, made some delightfully witty observations, but not once could I get to the emotion of it. *Raw Nerve* has taught me that comedians are hyper-attuned to "the laugh." They have made their living at it; it is what they are programmed to provide. Anything else is forbidden. He was a pro, and that finely tuned guard was not going to come down.

The show has been a hit for the Biography Channel, and the ratings have continued to grow with each season.

What did the critics say?

"[William Shatner] is surprisingly effective at getting his celebrity subjects to reveal aspects of their lives that are fresh and surprising."
—The Hollywood Reporter *(A fine publication; I get it delivered.)*
"Surprisingly sharp and intimate."—Newsday *(Hooray for* Newsday*! I always read it when I'm in New York.)*
"Nerve eschews the prototypical talk show format—Shatner's interview style is part Charlie Rose, part James Lipton, part

Dr. Phil."—USA Today *(A terrific paper—I love it when they drop it off outside my hotel room.)*

"This could be the freshest take on talk we've seen in a long time." —DISH Entertainment Magazine *(Haven't read it, but I would love to.)*

"Shatner's intense weirdness makes things compelling."—The New Yorker *(I dunno—some magazine that runs a lot of comics about talking dogs and psychiatrists.)*

From the Star Trek universe, I've interviewed Leonard Nimoy, LeVar Burton, Scott Bakula, and Walter Koenig. As I mentioned earlier, the interview with Walter was good for both of us and made for some great television.

I suppose no discussion of *Raw Nerve* is complete without talking about . . . the chair.

My talk show was going to be a different kind of talk show. I didn't want blue cards, I didn't want to prepare, I didn't want a sidekick (although I reconsidered that after meeting Jenna Jameson), and I sure as hell didn't want some boring old desk and a couch.

So I designed the S chair.

The S chair for me represents the whole show. We could not get any closer, any more personal, any more intimate. My guests are not even eighteen inches from my face. They must engage me, and *answer the questions.*

FUN FACTNER: William Shatner starred in a 1975 made-for-TV movie called *The Tenth Level*, which dramatized Stanley Milgram's obedience experiments. Shatner knows what he's doing when it comes to getting people to do what he wants them to do.

The S chair is almost a love seat. A love seat/hot seat! It's shaped like an S, with each participant facing the other in their respective S loops. Normally, such intimacy involving a chair will leave its occupants with a cleaning, several new fillings, and a new toothbrush. The only way *Raw Nerve* could be more intimate would be if I ditched the chair entirely and just replaced it with a bed.

Don't think I haven't thought about it. (See Jenna Jameson.)

But I decided to go with the chair. (See Meat Loaf.)

CHAPTER 21

RULE: Birds of a Feather Flock Together. But They Make for Dull Football Parties.

I mentioned earlier in *Shatner Rules* that I often hold salons at my house—evenings where creative thinkers from many fields get together and share ideas and philosophies. These are very enriching experiences for me.

But when I get tired of all that enrichment, I whip up some nachos, crack open a few beers, and throw football parties on Monday nights.

It's a tradition with me. There are about twenty guys who are regulars at my house for this, and the occasional special guest. I love to put different people together in the same room, and my football nights are a perfect vehicle for that. I mean, you will already be shouting at the screen—why not invite some guests who might encourage a little shouting at one another?

And after meeting him on the set of *Raw Nerve*, I decided that

Rush Limbaugh might be a pretty interesting guy to throw into the party mix. In many respects, I believe Rush is as much of a performer as I am, and I wanted to get to know this guy a little more. So I invited him to vacate the S chair at *Raw Nerve* and settle into one of the La-Z-Boys we have in our TV room.

I was taking a chance—Rush is a somewhat controversial figure. Especially in Hollywood. How would he behave at a football bash? Would he demand that the nachos show proof of citizenship? I kept my fingers crossed that things would get lively, but not too lively.

Rush showed up, and I introduced him around to the usual members of the gang. My buddy Fred Dryer, the former star of *Hunter* and former defensive end for the New York Giants and the LA Rams, stops by my football nights too. Having a real, honest-to-goodness professional football player watch and comment on games keeps the usual armchair sports bloviating at bay. Would it work on Rush?

Yep. Despite his brief stint in the NFL color booth for *Monday Night Football*, Rush left the analysis to Fred and was having a heck of a time. He's a fellow who really fills a room, and I could see he was really mixing in well with my usual gang.

And soon, another regular sauntered through the door. My other football buddy, Henry Rollins.

As previously mentioned, Henry is my pal from our work together on *Has Been*, and he has had an amazing career as punk rock singer, author, and spoken word artist. And before you sniff at "spoken word artist," you might take heed and Google a picture of him. If he didn't talk so much, his muscles could do his talking for him.

It is a pretty well-known fact that Henry is as liberal as Rush is conservative. In fact, he's so left wing and Rush is so right wing that I'm surprised they don't swing all the way around and bump into one another.

I was sitting with Rush, sharing a beer, when Henry entered. Being a regular, he walked over to the fridge to see if he could intimidate the appliance into giving him a beverage. I grabbed Rush by the sleeve and led him to the kitchen, determined to make this introduction.

"Henry," I said, switching into host mode, "have you met Rush Limbaugh?"

Henry pulled his head out of the fridge, his mouth agape. Rush smiled. Henry said nothing, and turned and stuck his head back into the fridge. It looked like a handshake was not in the offing.

Being a good host, I then attempted to distract Rush with a bowl of onion dip, and quickly brought him back to the couch.

Good Lord, football games are three hours long. How was I going to keep Rush and Henry separate?

Henry solved this dilemma by turning around and leaving the room, walking down the driveway, and getting into his car and taking off, shortly after my abortive introduction. Later, he left a voice mail on my machine:

"Hey, Bill, it's Henry. Sorry I left. I couldn't stand to be in the same room with that guy."

Apparently, Rush had found Henry's raw nerve, although I think if push had come to shove, Henry could have taken him.

I think those two need a little time in the S chair.

THIRD RULE FOR TURNING 80: YOU'RE 80. SAY WHAT'S ON YOUR MIND.

I f you've made it to eighty, congratulations are in order. You've worked hard, you've learned much, and the gleaming armor that protects your soul and spirit was forged in the mighty fires of wisdom!

Right?

Well, maybe. But if you're eighty, chances are you've at least picked up a few rich experiences along the way and have some opinions and passions.

I'm going to eschew the format of *Shatner Rules* for a bit and get serious about some serious stuff. No more rules, no more joking around.

How can I do that, you ask?

> **RULE: If You Make the Shatner Rules, You Get to Break the Shatner Rules**

What do I want to talk about as we break format?

Well, the thing I'm more than *always* happy to talk about is horses.

A.k.a. *Equus ferus cabbalus*, the large, hooved mammal that man has been domesticating for more than six thousand years, and a creature that has enchanted me for most of my life.

I have horses here in California, and I have them at my home in Kentucky. I keep them in both places. Seriously, horses are a real bitch to get into your carry-on.

For more than twenty years now, I have organized the Hollywood Charity Horse Show, where world-class reining horses and riders compete for top honors before a standing-room-only crowd. This year, we even live-streamed the event all over the world, an event that was topped off with a fantastic performance by Sheryl Crow. All the money we raise goes to my favorite charities, and to advance the science of hippotherapy.

Hippotherapy is a method of treating mental and physical handicaps with the sensory effects provided by interaction with horses. Often, it involves introducing mentally handicapped children to the wonders of the animal, wonders that elicit emotional responses from kids who don't respond to traditional therapy.

You wouldn't believe the transformation that takes place when some of these kids are placed atop an animal. Lately, Elizabeth has been spearheading an effort to bring hippotherapy to wounded veterans of our wars in Iraq and Afghanistan. Horses bring out the best in people, and they certainly bring out the best in me.

Also, if you are lucky enough to attend one of my Hollywood Charity Horse Shows, you will see me in a cowboy hat and boots. And you'll see me on horseback, competing in the reining events.

Reining is like figure skating on horseback, but without all the sequins. Although sometimes there are sequins—there's nothing wrong with being a little showy in the horse world. Reining is a competition where a horseman shows his skill in maneuvering the horse, doing what the cowboys did when driving cattle and herding calves.

Calves move fast, and they might dart to the right or to the left, so the cowboy might have to turn 180 degrees in either direction very fast on his horse. Figure skating has the double axel and the rocker foxtrot, while reining has the sliding stop, the rollback, the fast and slow circles, the change of leads. I practice these patterns every day when I'm riding, and I've become one of the top amateur reiners in the country.

Now, many actors have hobbies that take them out of the world of acting, and hobbies that have a tendency to take over their lives. My old friend and mentor Edward G. Robinson had a massive collection of abstract and impressionist art. Leonard Nimoy has all but abandoned acting for photography. Half the vehicles on the road in the city of Burbank belong to Jay Leno. (And Jay—can you put some turn signals on that Stanley Steamer? You nearly ran me off Ventura Boulevard the other day, damnit!)

Horseback riding won't take over acting, but to me, riding a horse is just like acting. As an actor, you need to forget your techniques; they must become second nature. The same thing goes for riding: The techniques of balance, placement of feet, where your hands are, where your mind-set is—it all vanishes when you enter the realm of horse riding. Like acting, horse riding is about seamless communication.

As an actor, if you know the words intrinsically, they're part of you. Once I'm up and going in a scene, I am no longer thinking of the words; I've got the words. You have to ride with this state of complete unity with the horse. You're into that Zen state of mind, body, and purpose. I have felt on numerous occasions that the horse's head and legs are my head and legs. I merely have to think and the horse does.

Would I give up acting to be with the horses full time? Of course not. I would never want horses to become my job. That would take the fun out of it.

And honestly, acting pays for the horses.

> **RULE: Being Eighty Means That You Can Abruptly Change the Subject While Speaking, and People Will Follow**

While I'm taking advantage of my elder statesman free rein, let's talk about the real rain. And how much acid is in it.

My own mortality is something that keeps me awake at night, but so does the mortality of this planet.

Heavy? Okay. But not as heavy as the destruction of the world.

When I first got concerned about the environment, there was

no jumping on the Hollywood bandwagon. Back then, the band-wagon was a one-seater, and I felt like the only one along for the ride. I read Rachel Carson's *Silent Spring*—the book that all but launched the modern American environmental movement—back in 1962, and it scared the living hell out of me. It should scare the living hell out of you, too. Especially those of you younger than eighty—you're gonna be stuck with this mess on Planet Earth longer than I will be.

Back in 1962, I would even try to bring up the environment in interviews, only to have reporters give me that "this is never going into my piece" look. I often felt like my character in the classic *Twilight Zone* episode "Nightmare at 20,000 Feet." I was shouting about impending disaster, but no one was listening. And the threats to our planet were and are much more severe than any from a man wearing a rubber suit shuffling around on an airplane wing.

Eventually, more people got on board over the years, and I try to be optimistic, but it takes more than sorting your recyclables and bringing your own bag to the grocery store. I fear we're doomed, and that within my grandchildren's lifetime, the conditions on our planet will be horrendous. And the main fight will be over water, not oil.

There are even potential disasters that aren't our doing. I've become acquainted with the fact that Yellowstone is rising. There's a giant magma bubble under Yellowstone that could blow at any moment, and if that were to happen, it would affect the whole of the western part of the United States. The potential for chaos and the Four Horsemen of the Apocalypse is only too real.

The destruction of the planet, and the lack of seriousness that our public representatives seem to be taking toward this destruction, troubles me deeply. We are not demanding their action. It is the nature of man to avoid thinking painful thoughts. We are naturally gifted in avoiding pain, whether it's physical or mental. *(NOTE: Another abrupt subject change ahead. I'm allowed. This is important.)*

This brings me back to my interest in mindful meditation, the thing that helps me get through a busy, four-Shatner day. Meditating: taking a moment to relax, allowing your muscles to unwind, to free your mind, to allow the thoughts to come, to focus on your breathing. I accept my fear for the world, and accept my resolve to do something about it, to warn others.

Mind you, all this meditation business doesn't mean that I'm "mellow." Not by any stretch. I still get a visceral feeling of anger when I see somebody throwing trash out the window of a car—a frequent sight here in Los Angeles.

When I see that, I will often drive up as close as I can to the driver and glower at them. If there's one benefit of living for eighty-plus years, it's that you've had plenty of time to work on your scowl. Unfortunately, the objects of my anger soon recognize the face that is expressing disdain, and then roll down their window, ask for an autograph, and herald, "Beam me up, Scotty!"

That's when they get the one-finger salute. After I give them the autograph.

I've been lucky enough to witness some of the more majestic sights nature has to offer and I want them to stay majestic. What can I say?

The foot of Mount Everest is one such majestic sight. In addition to some spectacular vistas of nature, this place also offers a glimpse into your soul.

I was in the Himalayas, sometime in the 1980s, staying at an ancient Buddhist temple, and I was looking for the spiritual epiphany that I've yearned for all my life. I've searched for it in my own way. Where are we going? What is life? What is the ultimate meaning of it all?

Like many before me, I felt the answer lay thousands of feet above sea level, in the freezing cold, with barely any plant life. There is also no air at all up that high on Everest—I would wake up at night, gasping for breath. Of course, I was sleeping outside.

That's right, the path to enlightenment does not involve a Sleeper King Suite at the Holiday Inn. Every evening, I would wrap myself up in the sleeping bag and sit outside in the dark night, waiting for the spirits of the mountains to enter my body or enter my soul or enter my consciousness, to speak to me in some manner.

And I'd wait day after day, night after night—and . . . nothing . . . until the wee hours of my last night in the bitter cold on the barren mountainside. I was leaving the following day, and I'd given up on making the big connection. I was sad. And shivering.

And suddenly, I was hit with an overwhelming wave of perception, a blinding flash of realization. I had finally acquired . . . the truth. My soul was opened and I was enlightened, and the enlightenment was this: that there exists nowhere on Earth a "soulful place," but that all, everywhere you are, is *the* soulful place. I could achieve what the Buddhist monks were trying to achieve in that valley at the confluence of Mount Everest and all those other holy mountains—wherever I was.

This entire world is filled with mystical qualities, including my little slice of the world, with its horses and dogs and loved ones, and that paradise and enlightenment are always within my reach. It's joy. And you should work on filling all your years with as much joy as possible. Even if you make it all the way to eighty and beyond.

Although honestly, I wish that wave of perception had come to me on the first night in Tibet. I would have hotfooted it to the nearest resort as soon as possible. Enlightenment can arrive in a hot tub, too.

CHAPTER 22

RULE: If You Go to the Land Down Under, Thumb It!

I should say that I'm not talking about hitchhiking. Australia is in the middle of nowhere, and it also contains thousands of square miles of nowhere in the middle of it. You do not want to get stuck without a lift in the bush—with or without a cardboard TWO MCGILL STUDENTS sign. A random dingo will gladly eat your baby, you, and whatever spare family members might be hanging around. You'll be down under, all right—six feet under!

RULE: Get the Australia Jokes out of the Way Early— Everyone's Heard 'Em Already

Australia is a rough-and-tumble nation full of wonderful, rough-and-tumble people. Open, loving, friendly, beautiful people. An Australian production company pitched me the idea of a touring night of anecdotes and stories, I agreed, and soon visited the great country in the spring of 2011 with my one-man show, *Kirk, Crane and Beyond: William Shatner Live.* (*$#*! My Dad Says* was also very popular there, but I thought the title *Kirk, Crane, and Other $#*!* might be a little too rough-and-tumble for even Australia.) Elizabeth and I happily made the journey to the faraway land, albeit one that felt slightly longer than my hitchhike across America as a teenager.

Kirk, Crane and Beyond: William Shatner Live was a two-hour-long program that featured me, a moderator (usually a local television or radio personality), tons of film clips, audience questions, and questions from the Twitterverse. We did shows in Sydney, Brisbane, and Melbourne, and then swung up to Auckland, New Zealand, to do a show there. In between, I also made it to a couple of Star Trek conventions. They are smaller than the American conventions, but people still come in costume. You can even hear Klingons sizing up one another's weapons à la Crocodile Dundee:

"Here—that's not a bat'leth. *That's* a bat'leth!"

Of course, when I perform live nowadays, like I did with *Kirk, Crane and Beyond*, it's not just jokes and anecdotes and questions answered. It's also songs!

And what do you sing when you tour Australia? Well, I know AC/DC heralds from down under, and perhaps on the next trip I will treat the crowd to my cover of "Hell's Bells," but during this tour, I performed two Australian classics: "Down Under," by Men at Work, and the unofficial national anthem, "Waltzing Matilda."

"Waltzing Matilda," in particular, was a real treat. It's the tale of a man in the bush, making a cup of tea, who poaches a sheep for his supper. When the authorities come to arrest him, he drowns himself in a water hole, and then haunts it for all eternity. (Actually, given its darker themes, perhaps AC/DC should do a cover of that song themselves.)

We decided to do "Waltzing Matilda" on the last show of the tour. There was no rehearsal, just me, a music stand, and our musical director on piano. He played, I interpreted, and the crowd ate it up. I really played up the drama of the song, and got to wrap my melodious diction around the following Australian words:

Swagman
Billabong
Jumbuck
Coolibah

I have to say that "billabong" and "coolibah" were my favorites, and I really . . . took . . . my . . . time . . . with . . . them. *(NOTE TO THE AUSTRALIANS IN THE AUDIENCE: I hope I pronounced all of the above properly, and I hope none of these terms are actually Australian curse words. If so, I'm sorry for all the obscenity.)*

As you might be able to tell from my last-minute interpretation of one of Australia's most beloved songs about billabongs, there was a great deal of working "without a net" on *Kirk, Crane and Beyond: William Shatner Live*. Improvising and riffing in front of an audience is one of my favorite things to do, and after a season of performing comedy live in front of a studio audience on *$#*! My Dad Says,* it is something I'd grown to relish.

But when working without a net, you sometimes forget there's a possibility that you might land on the hard concrete. Concrete soaking wet with fine, Australian beer. And it was at my Sydney show that I encountered an audience member who apparently thought *Kirk, Crane and Beyond* would be better after twelve or thirteen cans of Foster's Lager.

During our Q&A segment, people would step up to a microphone and ask whatever was on their mind. But at one point, some guy in the crowd starts shouting, "I got a question! Me, I got a question!" I told him to quiet down and wait his turn, but nothing doing.

In all my comedic experiences, this was the first time I've ever been heckled.

What are the typical responses to a heckler? I know there's always the reliable "Ahh, yes. I remember *my* first beer." But this was Australia—most people there experience their first beer from a plastic bottle with a nipple on it. That razor-sharp retort wouldn't work.

I've also heard, "I don't go to your job and knock over the Slurpee machine." Would Australians know what a Slurpee was? They know what a jumbuck is—they must have heard of a Slurpee.

Either way, before I could prepare a fittingly acerbic bon mot, he yelled out again, "I have a question!"

I yelled, "No, don't do that. You paid too much money for you to be talking and me to be talking. Let me do the talking. Also, there's a microphone. *That's* where you ask the questions."

RULE: When in Doubt, Go with the "Slurpee Machine" Comeback

Unfortunately, he stood up and began to lumber toward the mic. All six foot four inches of him. I was having Lee Van Cleef flashbacks. I was beginning to wonder if the organizers of a one-man show featuring an eighty-year-old actor had had the foresight to hire a security team.

He slurred, "My question is [unintelligible]."

Seriously. I couldn't understand what this deranged character was saying. He could have been shouting *Billabong!* for all I knew. (And for the purposes of recounting this story, I'll replace [unintelligible] with "billabong.")

I figured there was no assuaging him. "So what's your question?" I asked, hoping to keep him in the audience.

"Billabong," he sputtered, stepping on the feet of all the people in his row as he made his way toward the aisle. I figured it was time to get stern, take command, and negotiate. Give the crowd a dose of Kirk *and* Crane.

"Why don't you just sit back down and take it easy? Don't come this way because now you're being threatening."

He wasn't listening, and started walking down the aisle toward the stage. Kirk and Crane weren't cutting it. Time to go with Hooker.

"Do *not* come up on *my* stage."

Perhaps he'd never seen *T.J. Hooker*, because that's just what he did. And he began to shuffle toward me. What if he has a gun? I thought to myself. Since he was Australian, I just assumed he already had a knife on him. How on Earth was I to defuse this situation?

Lose Crane, Hooker, and just go full-on fighting Kirk? Without all the stuntmen backing me up? I knew some judo from the old days, had some knowledge of jujitsu, trained briefly in Krav Maga. Which discipline should I use to handle this sodden Aussie? One? Two? All three?

Or perhaps I could employ the ancient marital art of Running Away?

I sensed then that the moderator had gotten up and faded back to obtain the services of a police officer. I was grateful, but also thinking that William Shatner should handle any crisis that emerges during a William Shatner one-man show. A constable was procured, however.

As the cop began to head over to my visitor, I said, "No, leave him alone; it's okay," just as Mr. Billabong reached me on stage.

Once more with the Hooker.

"Sit down!" I snapped. And he obediently sat down.

Very obedient. Perhaps his inability to articulate came from being part dog? I didn't want to push my luck with "roll over," but it was tempting.

I'm standing over him and I instantly know that this is the best place for me to be. I've got the superior position now. I'm the star of this show and I'm in control.

"Okay, what is it you want to know?" I snapped.

"Billabong," he muttered.

"Speak clearly."

He was soused, and his bloodshot eyes scanned the crowd. "Farkus? Farkus? What's the question?" he yelled.

Farkus? I thought. *Who was that? Did this guy bring a friend?*

He obviously felt that clarity required a standing position, and he began to rise, grabbing my arm in the process. I could see the cop coming over now.

He was gripping my arm. This guy made contact with me. He crossed the line. It was time for . . .

The Thumb.

I don't know where I got this self-defense technique from—it's nothing Kirk ever employed—but I jabbed my thumb into his neck. Hard. Boom, he went down like a sack of swagmans.

"Stay down!" I ordered, keeping him—literally—under my thumb. He seemed surprised that I had detained him with only one digit, and sat there in his shock while the police officer came over and handcuffed him.

Handcuffs? Seems a little *easy*, don't you think, copper?

RULE: Make Fun of Australian Police Officers Only *after* You've Left Australia

I did have some personal, intimate contact with locals during my trip that I *did* appreciate, however. It was during my stop in Auckland, New Zealand. The show was going to run just like the Australian shows—without the seven-minute-long standoff with a drunk and his buddy Farkus—but with the inclusion of a new song called "Welcome Home," which I was to perform with Kiwi singer Dave Dobbyn and performer Whirimako Black.

Dobbyn is a very popular performer in his native New Zealand, and in 2002 he became an officer of the New Zealand Order of Merit for his talent and contributions to the music world there. Whirimako Black is Maori and a popular singer who often performs in the traditional language over traditional melodies. She too, is a member of the New Zealand Order of Merit. The organizers of this show were clearly pulling out the heavy guns for my performance. It was a little intimidating.

Before the show, Dobbyn and Black came backstage to meet me and go over the song a bit. Ms. Black's face was lined with the traditional *ta moko* Maori tattoo, an important and striking cultural symbol of the indigenous peoples. She had a request.

"Mr. Shatner. My mother loved you when she was alive. May I hug you for her? My mother would have loved to have held you."

I was more than willing to oblige such a wonderful and meaningful request. Sure beats your average, run-of-the-mill "Can I have your autograph?"

And it was a long hug, a silent hug, and one that she was doing so that the spirit of her departed mother could experience it. People were in my dressing room, watching us, but they all receded far, far away into the background. The only thing I could hear was my breath, her breath, and perhaps the breath of her lost mother.

Soon, I began to cry, and so did she. By the end of our hug, I was sobbing.

"Welcome home," indeed.

And if my drunken Australian friend is reading this—*that's* how you handle a William Shatner meet and greet!

QUIZ

Which one of these is an Australian slang word, and which is a character once played on a TV show by William Shatner?

A. Bascom   D. Manoshma

B. Kovalik   E. Bodosh

C. Gronke   F. Rawhide MacGregor

Actually, they are *all* the names of characters I've played in such TV shows or TV movies as *TekWar*, *The Horror at 37,000 Feet*, *Sole Survivor*, and *Route 66*.

The answer for option F is "both." I once played the character Rawhide MacGregor in the TV movie *North Beach and Rawhide*, and in Australia, a "Rawhide MacGregor" is a condition suffered by outback sheepherders when they've been sitting in the saddle for too long.

CHAPTER 23

RULE: Dying Is Easy. Dying on Stage While Doing Comedy Is Easy, Too.

For many years in Hollywood, when an agent got a comedy script tossed onto his or her desk, the first phone call they made usually wasn't to William Shatner.

If they needed a crusading district attorney, a race-baiting zealot, noted Roman statesman Marc Antony, a honeymooner who becomes enslaved by a fortune-telling machine, a Swedish farmer squaring off with Lee Van Cleef, a brother named Karamazov, a young sailor named Billy Budd—you gave William Shatner a call. You didn't call him if you needed a clown.

Heck, I was even hired to play a Burmese sailor named Maung Tun on an episode of the old police show *Naked City*. But I just couldn't book comedy. (Although someone in the casting department at *Naked City* clearly had a sense of humor, booking a Canadian as a Burmese sailor.)

This is ironic because I spent most of my time in college and in repertory acting in comedies, like *The Seven Year Itch*. But once I landed on the New York stage, started doing television, and then films, I could not be taken seriously as a clown.

This is too bad, because I love comedy, and love performing comedy. And I'm glad that the second half of my career has allowed me more opportunities to make people laugh. And again that's laugh *with*, not *at*.

Performing comedy is like performing a knife-throwing act at a sideshow: When done properly it can amaze and awe, but one mistake, and there's blood on the stage. Comedy is like an orchid: When tended to properly, it is a thing of beauty, but when it's not, it withers and dies. Comedy is like chocolate soufflé: With careful monitoring it can rise to great heights, but if you slam the door too hard—flat as an unfunny pancake.

RULE: Comedy Comes in Threes. So Do My Metaphors.

If you had asked me a few years ago, "What's the purest form of acting?" I would have said "theater!" But after my experience on *$#*! My Dad Says,* I have to say that it's sitcom acting. There's a communication and concentration required that is unlike anything I have ever experienced as a performer.

On a sitcom, you need to communicate with your audience and concentrate on what you're doing. In drama, so many different opinions matter: the director's, the producers', the writers', and so on and so on. In comedy, ultimately, the most important opinion is the audience's.

Doing comedy in front of an audience is like a juggling act (oops, sorry, I maxed out my metaphor limit). It's all timing, and it becomes all rhythm. If somebody coughs in the audience, it screws up the laugh. If you have the slightest hesitation on a word—if you hesitate, if you can't think of the perfect bon mot, the comedic moment is gone and the audience always knows it.

The people who came to see *$#*! My Dad Says* had a tremendous impact on the show and on my performance. We would run a scene in front of the crowd, and if I failed to connect, they wouldn't laugh. When they didn't laugh, our producers, Max Mutchnick and David Kohan, would round up the writers and we'd try the scene again—but with different punch lines. Each thirty-minute episode was a mutual collaboration between performer, writer, and audience—more so than in any other genre.

In doing comedy you have to listen, you have to adjust, but most important, you . . . have . . . to . . . take . . . your . . . time.

A favorite comedian of mine was Dick Shawn, and he really personified both the ecstasy and the agony of comedy for me. I once went to see him perform in the mid 1980s. My wife and I arrived early, sat down in the auditorium, and noticed a large pile of paper and debris on the stage. I couldn't figure out if it was part of the set dressing, or some garbage they forgot to remove from a previous performance.

Either way, time passed, about twenty minutes or so, as people filled in to take their seats. Suddenly the lights went down, a voice came over the PA announcing, "Ladies and gentlemen—Dick Shawn!," and Shawn leapt up from the pile of garbage.

He had been waiting there, silent, for nearly half an hour, just for that big, crazy laugh of surprise.

Patience. What a virtue.

Shawn was a master of taking his time. He would do these long, rambling jokes—with laugh-free setups—that wouldn't pay off until the very end. I so admired his courage—what if the joke tanked? As they say in comedy, "That's a long way to go to find out that the store is closed." Audiences hate it when they feel their time has been wasted. But Shawn was fearless.

In fact, his commitment was such that when he was performing at a show in San Diego in 1987, he was doing a joke about the end of the world when he did a face-plant on the stage. The audience roared. And Shawn did not get up. The audience kept laughing.

It had to be part of the joke, right? This was the guy who was known to hide under a pile of trash for thirty minutes just to get an opening laugh. And the audience was patient until the paramedics arrived.

Shawn had had a massive, fatal heart attack while performing.

Needless to say, I really admired Dick Shawn's timing and patience and courage, but no comedian should ever die like that on stage.

And I was thinking about him in 2005, when I was invited by the American Film Institute to celebrate the bestowing of a very special lifetime achievement honor. And even when I discovered that I wasn't the honoree, I consented to stick around.

Who was the man of the hour? George Lucas.

The highlight of Lucas's career was probably when he was the cameraman on a religious anthology program I once acted on called *The Psalms*. But he's done other stuff too, like *American Graffiti* and the *Star Wars* movies.

FUN FACTNER: You can purchase *The Psalms* at WilliamShatner.com. It's the perfect gift for that family member who loves William Shatner, George Lucas, and the word of God.

Now, lifetime achievement awards are taken very seriously in Hollywood. In fact, most everything to do with awards in Hollywood is taken very seriously. If you want to suck the air out the room at any Oscars celebration, get on stage and make some barbed comments about the nominees. Do you remember who won the Golden Globes last year? Of course you don't—but I'm sure you remember the furor Ricky Gervais caused after his caustic monologue full of showbiz attacks hit the air.

And now I was tasked to open this special event . . . this lifetime honor to one of the most successful and powerful men in film . . . with some comedy. But not just a series of one-liners. I had to go out there and take my time and do a character bit and lead the audience to the laugh. An audience perhaps not in the mood to laugh. After all, they were in the presence of a master. One who could put them in his movies! It was a very serious moment.

This was a black-tie, top-tier event. In addition to Lucas, the crowd was filled with such luminaries as Harrison Ford, Steven Spielberg, Warren Beatty, Robert Duvall, and Chewbacca!

Yes, Chewbacca was seated near the stage. I think he even had a better seat than his costars, Mark Hamill and Carrie Fisher. *(NOTE TO CHEWBACCA: Don't wear your ammo belt to a black-tie event. The tabloids will put you in a "fashion don'ts" spread, and rightfully so.)*

The banquet room was decorated with—needless to say—a *Star Wars* theme. There were massive posters, pictures, even an X-wing fighter hung from the ceiling. And the first person anyone was going to see on stage?

That dude from *Star Trek*.

"Ladies and gentlemen, please welcome . . . William Shatner."

Can you say "cognitive dissonance?"

I walked out, and the crowd was . . . puzzled. The response somewhat . . . muted. I felt like I had stepped into a rumble between *Twilight* and *Harry Potter* fans in the middle of ComicCon. *(NOTE: Referring to elements of recent popular culture will help gain hip young readers. Thanks again, grandkids!)*

I could see George Lucas on his special dais, sandwiched between Spielberg and Ford, looking baffled. And I could see Mr. Han Solo himself mouth the words, "What? The? Fuck?" (Clearly I elicit that response. Perhaps that should have been the title of *Shatner Rules*?)

Even Chewbacca folded his arms, and roared, "Bring it, bitch!" *(NOTE: I am not fluent in Wookie.* Star Wars *is for nerds.)*

I got to the middle of the stage and felt a tad nervous. When you're nervous, the instinct is to rush. Get it done. Get off the stage, run back to your car, and go home.

But no. I had to be patient. My comedy needed its knife thrown, its orchid watered, its soufflé fluffed. I was going to take . . . my . . . time.

I smiled and said, "Ladies and gentlemen. *Star Trek* changed everything."

Totally unexpected, out of left field, a tad disrespectful? It got a laugh, but not a giant laugh, and about half of it was nervous laughter. Lucas seemed confused. I was starting to sweat. Did I want to bomb in front of Steven Spielberg? Of course not. But I stuck with it.

Patience. Again, the key.

I looked around the room, admired all the sci-fi decoration, and declared ". . . and aren't these conventions wonderful?"

Boom. There was the laugh. Lucas even laughed. Chewbacca nodded and gave a thumbs-up (I didn't know Wookiees had thumbs). They were finally with me.

I pretended to be confused, and then slowly pulled a piece of paper out of my pocket and began to read it.

"Dear Mr. Shatner . . . we'd love to have you open the show . . . Star *Wars*?!?!"

I was milking it, and the audience was eating it up.

"Wait a minute, I can do *Star Wars*," I corrected, as I stared into Mr. Lucas's eyes. "George . . . it's George, isn't it? May I call you George? You can call me Mr. Shatner."

Laughs and more laughs. Had I rushed it, had I bailed, the whole bit would have bombed and wound up on the cutting room floor, replaced with a montage of scenes from *The Psalms* and other Lucas masterpieces.

Eventually, my bit ended with me singing "My Way" and doing a kick line with a bunch of Storm Troopers. I even gave a shout-out to Chewbacca, who then stood up and fist pumped.

I was patient, took my time, read the crowd, and got the laughs. Comedy is a delicate, wonderful thing.

And now, I'm waiting—patiently—for the call from either Lucas or Spielberg. It's been six years now since the show. Come on, guys. I can do comedy. I can even throw knives, if that's what you really want.

CHAPTER 24

RULE: Settle for Second Billing Only If the Top-Billed Act Can Beat You Up

RESERVED FOR

METALLICA

WILLIAM SHATNER

That's what a little sign read on the table in my tented VIP cabana at the Nokia Theater in downtown Los Angeles. There was no sign of this so-called Metallica, but if they were going to get higher billing than me, I was going to take their goody bags. (My grandkids *love* guitar picks, Linkin Park T-shirts, and studded leather wrist bracelets.)

I was at the Revolver Golden Gods Awards, where I was to receive the coveted Honorary Headbanger Award. A headbanger is a heavy metal or hard rock fan who rocks his or her head violently back and forth while listening to said music.

(NOTE: Please—don't ask me to ever demonstrate. I am an honorary head-banger. I am not licensed to head bang, nor may I practice it, or advise others on its practice. At least not in the state of California. But if you ask me in Nevada—let's rock!)

I settled down into my chair in the little "Metallica and Me" section, ordered a beer and some sliders, and gazed at the crowd. A parade of young—and not so young—metalheads, tattooed and bestudded, passed me by, occasionally stopping to do a double take at the sight of Mr. and Mrs. William Shatner. It was quite a bizarre crowd. The VIP room was a who's who of "what the hell is that?"

(NOTE: Give yourself extra time when attending a headbanger awards banquet. It takes forever to get through the metal detectors.)

I usually ask myself this a couple of times a week, and while sitting there drowning in the sonic assault of the speakers at this heavy metal melee, I pondered, *How did I get here?*

But I guess music has always been part of my life in a way. When I was a child, my father would come home from his clothing business on Saturdays and put the Metropolitan Opera broadcast from New York on the radio. I would often close my eyes and wonder what the singers looked like. (I doubt they looked anything like the singers on the black carpet at the Golden Gods Awards. Those fat ladies at the opera could sing, but none of them could wail like these metalheads.) In college, I directed some musicals, and even took some voice lessons as a young actor. And now, at the age of eighty, I have three full-length records under my belt.

Yes, three. *The Transformed Man, Has Been*, and . . . *Searching for Major Tom*. It's in record stores now. You might want to purchase it and listen to it while reading this book. (Headbanging while reading keeps you from looking too nerdy.)

Searching for Major Tom started in 2010 when the head of Cleopatra Records, Brian Perera, visited my office. He sat on the very couch that once held the Foos Brothers when we began discussions of *Has Been*.

"We'd love for you to sing on an album for us," he asked.

"I don't sing," I replied.

"Oh, I know. But sing—like you do—on an album of science fiction songs."

I began to look for a way to wrap up the conversation quickly. I explained that I didn't want to do an album of science fiction–themed tunes. Would I be holding a toy laser gun on the front cover? Would the songs be punctuated by sound effects? This had "novelty" written all over it, not worth my time.

Brian thanked me, and left some sheet music on my desk for these "science fiction songs." Later, I began to go over some of the lyrics. One was "Space Oddity" by David Bowie, which—judging from Bowie's ever-changing appearance over the years—I assumed was autobiographical.

But no, it was about a character named Major Tom. And he

appeared in more than one of the songs on my desk. He is the title character in a song by Peter Schilling, there was another tune called "Mrs. Major Tom," and then there was the sheet music to Elton John's "Rocket Man," which is basically about Major Tom.

FUN FACTNER: William Shatner became one of the first artists to cover "Rocket Man" when he performed it at the Saturn Awards in 1978.

SECONDARY ADDITIONAL FUN FACTNER: Cee Lo sent a thank-you note after William Shatner became one of the first artists to cover "Fuck You." Are you reading this, Elton John?

It occurred to me then that this didn't have to be a novelty album full of random sci-fi songs; it could be a *concept* album that tells a story, much like *Has Been* and *The Transformed Man*. This could be an opportunity to blow some minds. And—if we got the right musicians on board—blow some speakers.

Searching for Major Tom began to take shape once Adam Hamilton hopped on board as producer. We began to tell a story of an astronaut at a crossroads in his life, while deep in outer space. And we began to assemble songs and artists who would help me tell the story.

What are the songs? Who are the artists? We recorded Deep Purple's "Space Truckin'," with Johnny Winter on guitar—one of *Rolling Stone* magazine's 100 Greatest Guitarists of All Time—and "She Blinded Me with Science" with Bootsy Collins on bass, a man who has spent plenty of time in the outer reaches of the universe. I cover U2's "In a Little While." Michael Schenker from the Scorpions rocks like a hurricane with me on Tea Party's "Empty Glass." I croon "Lost in the Stars" with jazz great Ernie Watts on sax. I cover Golden Earring's "Twilight Zone," which has nothing to do with gremlins on planes or guys obsessed with fortune machines.

"Space Cowboy" by Steve Miller? I do it, with my pal Brad Paisley (he provides the cowboy, I handle the space). Peter Frampton comes alive on a version of Norman Greenbaum's "Spirit in the Sky," while two of the loudest musicians ever—guitarist Wayne Kramer (from the MC5) and drummer Carmine Appice (who has been in nearly ever band that ever was)—back me up on Hawkwind's "Silver Machine."

You indie rock types will "dig" (am I using that right?) the Strokes' Nick Valensi's work on "Major Tom," while classic metal fans can "jam" (not sure about that one) with Deep Purple's Ritchie Blackmore on our cover of "Space Oddity." Alan Parsons plays on that one, too, taking time off from his Project.

I land on Duran Duran's "Planet Earth" with Steve Howe from Yes, I "Walk on the Moon" with Toots of Toots and the Maytals, Dave Davies from the Kinks helps me blast off with the Byrds'

"Mr. Spaceman," and I was "Learning to Fly" with my own take on the latter-day Pink Floyd classic. Together, we put all these songs together to make a real rock opera. And unlike *Tommy*, you don't need to be stoned to figure out what *Searching for Major Tom* is about.

Who else is on the album? Mike Inez from Alice in Chains, John Wetton from Asia, Edgar Froese from Tangerine Dream, guitarist Steve Hillage, keyboardist Patrick Moraz, Manuel Gott-sching from Ash Ra Tempel, Warren Haynes from the Allman Brothers Band and Gov't Mule, and the lovely Sheryl Crow. Plus too many others to mention.

In putting this project together, Adam Hamilton, along with music industry heavy-hitter John Lappen, brought me my own Rock and Roll Hall of Fame. It truly rocked.

Have you ever heard "Bohemian Rhapsody" by Queen and said to yourself, "I wish William Shatner would perform this." Well, wish no more! I cover it on this album. The whole thing! Queen liked long songs—they must have been fans of *The Transformed Man*. I found the whole thing *magnifico*! And Galileo! Even Figaro!

The second to last song on the album is "Iron Man" by Black Sabbath. In the context of our album, this song represents hell to Major Tom, who is teetering on the brink of life and death.

I went into the studio with Adam and laid down my vocals for this blackest of Black Sabbath tracks, and then stepped back into the bright light of Los Angeles and went on my way.

But a few weeks later, Adam called me and wanted me to hear the guitar track that Zakk Wylde had laid down for the song.

Have you heard of Zakk Wylde? (My spell-check program hasn't.) He is one of America's preeminent hard rock guitarists. He played alongside Ozzy Osbourne for many years, and now fronts his own heavy metal band, Black Label Society. He's this massive, scary-looking guy with long hair and a long, braided beard. I don't think he has ever worn a shirt with sleeves.

And when I heard his guitar work, *I* was transformed.

It was raw. It was powerful. It was . . . fucking gnarly. (I *must* be using that one right, right?)

So raw, in fact, that I went back in the studio to re-record my "Iron Man" vocals. I had to do justice to the blistering, six-string assault created by Zakk's Gibson Les Paul.

Bill kicks some serious ass recording his version of Black Sabbath's "Iron Man" for his newest album in 2011.

My original track wasn't dirty enough. It wasn't Ozzy Osbourne, it was Ozzie Nelson. (Ask your grandparents, kids.) I needed to scream.

While screaming, I realized that heavy metal is nothing more than raw energy. That's what defines it. And I needed to tap into that energy with all my might. My voice is very important to me, but that afternoon, all I cared about was screaming—voice be damned.

FUN FACTNER: Recording *Searching for Major Tom* is the reason there was almost a *$#*! My Dad Says* episode called "Ed Needs a Lozenge."

I began to school myself in the metal arts. There is now Iron Maiden on my iPod. They are one of the few artists on my iPod. And they have so far made nice with the assorted jazz tunes and NPR podcasts I've downloaded. Although I think *Fear of the Dark* can most certainly beat up *A Prairie Home Companion*.

RULE: Keep Your *Prairie Home Companion* References to a Minimum While Promoting Your Heavy Metal Album

And with the album done, I found myself in a stretch limousine, headed off to the Golden Gods Awards. I didn't know what awaited me. Elizabeth and I wore black, I knew that much. And I tried to prep for all the questions I'd be asked on the black carpet.

QUESTIONS ASKED OF WILLIAM SHATNER ON THE BLACK CARPET OF THE REVOLVER GOLDEN GODS AWARDS

Why are you here?

What are you doing here?

Why the hell are you here?

Do *you* know where you are?

Seriously, why are you here?

Do you know where I can get my parking validated, dude?

I eventually made it down the carpet, enjoyed a long interview with former Skid Row frontman Sebastian Bach, posed for pictures with Sebastian Bach, and then later entertained more questions from Sebastian Bach. Dude's got a mancrush!

Eventually we made it to my shared Metallica waiting area. They still hadn't showed up when it was time for me to be presented with my award. Elizabeth took the RESERVED FOR METALLICA/ WILLIAM SHATNER sign as a souvenir. That's a pairing that shouldn't happen. There is such a thing as "too" metal.

Backstage, it occurred to me that I hadn't prepared a speech. This was unlike me, especially after lecturing Ben (fold) Folds about preparation and punctuality. I began to go over a few of the things I could say to win over the crowd of metalheads.

"I have gone where no man has gone before. And tonight—I go to eleven!"

"There's a hearse in the parking lot with its lights on, license plate 666."

"All hail Satan!"

I had nothing, and then they called my name. The crowd roared.

And they roared metal. Raw, uninhibited, pure energy. Before me was a sea of people, men and women, all clad in black with leather, spikes, and studs everywhere, cheering me on.

Had any of them ever spent a Saturday afternoon listening to the Metropolitan Opera with their father? Who knows—maybe? All music has the power to unite people. And metal has united these people strong. They are welded to the sound.

I finally got to the mic, and all I could feel was the energy and emotion of the crowd. I was handed my statue (of Stonehenge—a tribute to Spinal Tap), I raised it aloft and shouted . . .

"FUCKING GNARLY!"

I think I was using it right.

FOURTH RULE FOR TURNING 80: GET. OUT. OF. BED.

And this may be the most important rule of all. You don't necessarily have to be eighty for it to be important. But if you are eighty, it is something you must do.

When I turned forty, I didn't get out of bed for three days.

Forty was tough. I was divorced. I was often not employed to the level I wanted to be. I had just come off the road from touring in summer stock and dinner theater productions, living out of a truck.

Not "living out of a truck" the way one "lives out of a suitcase." I was living in a truck. With my dog. When I would travel from town to town, I would shower inside the theater, perform, greet the fans, and then go to bed in a truck. Clearly my finances were not what they should have been.

RULE: You Can't Be a Swinging Bachelor If Your Bachelor Pad Gets Towed for Being Too Close to a Hydrant

It's hard being broke when you're an actor. In most any other profession, if you hit rock bottom, if you've spent your last dime, you can shift gears without anyone noticing. I was drained financially after my divorce settlement, and I couldn't hide, couldn't shift gears.

"Hey, that temp in accounting? Didn't he used to be on that *Star Trek* show? Tell him to beam up my expense reports."

As an actor, you might have made next to nothing on your last movie, but you had better show up to the premiere dressed to the nines or, as Hollywood often demands, dressed to the tens. Nobody wants to hear that 10 percent of your earnings went to your agent, another 10 to your lawyer, and maybe even 15 went to your manager and the other 65 percent to your ex-wife. They just demand you be famous and appear famous.

The best way to be successful in Hollywood is to seem successful, no matter the cost. The sweet smell of success can overpower the stench of failure.

Thankfully, forty years later, I'm in much better shape. Daniel Ellsberg mentioned to me while taping our *Raw Nerve* interview that miracles happen all the time—miracles are just the things that happen that you don't expect. I wish I could go back in time and share Ellsberg's wisdom with the forty-year-old me.

Eighty is great. I'm married, financially secure, and have work whenever I want it.

But here's the thing . . .

When I woke up on my fortieth birthday, I felt like my career was over. That was terrible.

When I woke up on my eightieth birthday, I felt that might life might be over soon. That was terrifying.

I thought I was prepared for March 22, 2011. What is eighty, other than a number? I'm in good shape; all the horse riding has been great for my legs and my upper body strength. I feel great; I take my vitamins and exercise every day. (I don't use skin creams or cosmetics, though. I'm an actor, but I'm not *that* much of an actor.)

But the terror of dying felt very keen that morning in the darkness of my bedroom.

God, I'm going to die. Very soon, I thought to myself. Everyone knows they are going to die, no matter how much they deny it, but once you're eighty, you're now actually on a deadline.

Elisabeth Kübler-Ross outlines the five stages of grief in her book *On Death and Dying.* They are denial, anger, bargaining, depression, and acceptance. I had already jumped to my own "acceptance," and I hadn't even gotten out of my pajamas yet.

> **RULE: Do Not Keep Elisabeth Kübler-Ross on Your Nightstand.** *Shatner Rules* **Is a Slightly Lighter Read.**

There are some people who view death as an adventure. I once heard that Timothy Leary's last words were, "Of course." At the moment of death he saw the logic of the universe. What a joyous celebration of the unknown! That line alone offers me more comfort than any one of the supposed five people you meet in Heaven.

You know who else saw death as an adventure?

Kirk.

I never played Kirk with fear. Kirk was never frightened; he was always amazed, curious. And that's how I approached his death, once it became clear that the executives at Paramount were hell bent on killing him off.

What would Captain Kirk feel at the moment of death, having lived his life looking at the strangest animals and the strangest things?

Captain Kirk would look at death with awe and wonder. He wouldn't run from it; he would move forward toward it. I imagined that Captain Kirk would look at whatever death is—blackness, lightness, the devil, God, nothing—and wonder *Where am I going?* without fear. *I'm on another step on the journey. What's the next step after this one?*

Kirk's final words upon his death in *Star Trek: Generations* were, "Oh my." No fear. No fear at all!

So, this attitude of Kirk's can be used to prove one thing, once and for all.

I am not Captain James T. Kirk.

On my eightieth birthday, I just lay there in my terror, no awe or wonder to be found. I wish I could stampede over to a belief system that offered me a convenient afterlife and a benevolent God. That kind of thing requires faith, and I don't have it. I would love to be nurtured in the arms of someone ecclesiastical when I die, but I don't think that's going to happen.

The fear that I had that morning marking my eightieth year comes from the loneliness in all of our souls; this is the promontory that every human being stands on. We yearn to be joined with someone or something. We strive all our lives to do so with marriage and children and friends and family and clans and country and patriotism and pets—yes, pets—and even sometimes objects that aren't alive, statues, concepts like God, cults. Whatever.

But even in the holiest of holy people, I have to think that deep down there exists doubt. That doubt is in me, it consumes me. *We're all alone; in the end, we're all alone,* I thought in my bed on the first morning of my eightieth year. *And you have to suffer through those feelings by yourself.*

Elizabeth rolled over and wished me a happy birthday.

RULE: Marry Someone Who Remembers Your Birthday

I might not believe in the standard view of God. I might not believe in an afterlife. But I most certainly believe in love. There's proof of it. It's all around me, I can touch it, and I can experience it. It will protect me from the existential terror of my failure to exist.

It finally occurred to me—when I turned forty, I could afford three days to lie in bed. At eighty—I don't have that luxury. The clock keeps ticking.

Get. Out. Of. Bed.

Even if you're lying in bed next to Elizabeth, one of the greatest individuals I've ever encountered. She is enormously kind and has a great capacity for love. She's highly intelligent, has a great sense of humor, and is very empathetic. She understands so much.

And she throws a great party.

Toward the end of the run of *Boston Legal*, Denny Crane was given a great line: "I live my life as though I'm in a television show." That one hits home. I've been coming into people's homes for nearly sixty years now, and I'm not quite ready for cancellation. So let's cue the music, and

CUT TO · INT · SHATNER HOME
MARCH 22, 2011 · FADE IN:

We see WILLIAM SHATNER, 80—not ready to fade out—surrounded by loved ones, smiling.

Elizabeth really does throw a great party. We were surrounded with friends, family, and my dogs, Starbuck and Cappuccino (who thankfully decided not to tear up their doggy beds for the occasion). Elizabeth even hired a drum circle.

And it was a drum circle indoors, because there was a monsoon outside. If there is a God, I think he was jealous of all the fun I was having.

There's a song I wrote for *Has Been* called "It Hasn't Happened Yet." It sums up perfectly those feelings of loneliness and failure that have chased me all my life.

> *As the carillon sang its song*
> *I dreamt of success.*
> *I would be the best.*
> *I would make my folks proud.*
> *I would be happy . . .*
>
> *—It hasn't happened yet*
> *—It hasn't happened yet*
> *—It hasn't happened*

Among my many gifts was a plate from Elizabeth, which bore the legend IT HAPPENED.

As the party and evening progressed, the storm grew even more violent; it felt like the afterparty the night of the Golden Gods Awards. We were all in a tent, and the drumming of the rain threatened to drown out the drumming of the drummers. The hillside behind my house began to collapse, trees began to fall.

Would this army of love around me protect me from the elements, from the unknown, from certain disaster, and despair, and loneliness? From the dark specter of inevitable death?

As Timothy Leary might say, "Of course."

Besides, how can I die when I have so many lifetime achievement awards to collect?

CHAPTER 25

RULE: Don't Die. You'll Miss Out on All the Lifetime Achievement Awards.

I don't know why more people don't follow this rule. Seriously, dying is a bore! And lifetime achievement awards are a lot of fun.

In June of 2011, I was invited to McGill University in Montreal, my alma mater, so that I could accept an honorary Ph.D. As with my Honorary Headbanger Award, I am more than aware of the limitations of the title. Only in symbolic medical emergencies may I assist, and I will only be allowed to rhetorically defend any of my make-believe dissertations.

McGill, this storied institution of learning, has been very good to me over the years, despite the fact that my title of "academic slacker" while attending was anything but symbolic. While matriculated, I felt that my learning needed to be done outside the classroom, although if I had ever deigned to *enter* a classroom in my four-plus years of going there, I might have found book learning appealing.

The university has produced seven Nobel Prize winners, Pulitzer Prize winners, and Academy Award winners, and I'm sure you can find out all about their histories if you ask around at the William Shatner University Centre.

Yep, the student union is named after me, thanks to a student referendum in 1992. Traditionally, buildings at McGill have been named after benefactors or dead people. Last time I checked, I'm neither. I am furiously avoiding death and—as for the money— well, McGill, I put the check in the mail. It must have gotten lost.

RULE: Nobody Buys "The Dog Ate My Endowment Check" Excuse Anymore

An honorary doctorate! Not bad for a kid who barely graduated high school and who entered McGill thanks to a Jewish quota

Bill takes his chapeau off to his alma mater, McGill University, in Montreal in 2011.

program. Keep in mind, McGill was also giving an honorary degree to publishing magnate and fellow Jew Mort Zuckerman, so at least I know that *my* degree was not filling some sort of cultural requirement.

So there I was, in my jaunty cap and gown, standing before the graduates. Years ago, I hadn't graduated with my own class because I had to make up some courses I'd failed. This ceremony would be my first official graduation. Eventually, it came time for me to share my honorary wisdom with the students, and I read a speech I prepared. This is what I said.

(NOTE: If you would like to experience what it was really like to be a graduate listening to William Shatner speak, pretend to worry about your job prospects, and start rehearsing your breakup speech to your college girlfriend/boyfriend.)

This was an easy degree to get. Just say "yes" and they hand you a degree. Thank you very much. While I am honored and grateful, it wasn't quite so easy getting my bachelor degree of commerce from McGill.

I had quite a struggle actually—first getting into McGill, it being such a prestigious university. My academics weren't all that good coming out of West Hill High School, which is now defunct. The only vivid memory I have of West

Hill High was corporal punishment, where the teachers whipped you with a rubber mallet on your open palm if you had done something requiring punishment, like coming late to classes—which I did—or being rambunctious within the classroom—which I did—or even burning the principal's car—which someone else did and I deny it to this day! But the only thing that remains more vivid than anything else is that we won the city championships. We became a dynasty. We won several football championships, and I was really the best player on the second team—the story of my life.

So when I came to McGill, I earnestly thought that I could be the best football player on the second team of the freshman class. After all, I weighed 160 pounds and could run the one-hundred-yard dash in something like fourteen seconds flat. Slow but sure—the story of my life.

Sadly, I didn't make the freshman football team. Somebody punched me in the stomach and then somebody else stepped on my head. You can imagine I didn't do so well with the breakfast I had eaten a little earlier, making my first day my last day. It was then that I discovered drama. Things would have to be easier at university, so I joined the drama club. But not really.

I had been active in amateur theatricals for several years before that, on radio and on stage, with television yet to be invented. That's how far back I go, folks.

And when I came to McGill, I followed those interests and became at some point president of the Radio Club and a creative force on the Red White and Blue, performing university musicals. It was through creating those musicals that I got my university education.

In a student union building, a couple blocks from the present student union building, in the basement, under the stairs, the Red White and Blue had their offices. Their offices consisted of a desk, a chair, and a sofa. I made better use of the sofa than the desk. That's a whole other education I received.

(NOTE: At this point, I attempted to run up and down the aisles, administering high fives. Under threats of having my degree revoked by the dean, I returned to the stage.)

My point is that my academic life at McGill—where I was working on a bachelor of commerce degree with all of those accounting, economics, and mathematics classes, none of which I attended because I was too busy trying to clean the sofa in the Red White and Blue office—wasn't easy.

In those days, there were very few vacuum cleaners and spray cleaners—it was all done by hand—another part of my university education. But what this did teach me was not only cleanliness but also hard work. Running around that desk in the Red White and Blue office was hard work. I felt the sweat on my face running around that desk. It taught me that if you wanted to get something done, you had to get up early in the morning. When asked what my secret is to being successful, my answer has always been get up earlier in the morning. There is nothing that you can't accomplish when standing on two feet. When you are lying down, all you accomplish is some REM sleep and working out your dream life.

When I graduated, which I did just barely in the fall after I made up a half course in math, which I had failed, I got my degree. In September I landed my first professional job in a small acting company in Montreal at Mount Royal.

The bothersome thing was that I got the job as an assistant manager by telling them I got a bachelor of commerce degree and I was adept at accounting and banking. This was the only other lie I ever told. The first one being that I hadn't set fire to the principal's car. It wasn't long before they discovered two things: that I had no accounting skills whatsoever—my math skills are really bad—and that I was a good actor.

My talents didn't lie in the field of accounting. My father, who paid for my education, was not amused. But my talents lay in trying to be funny and entertaining people. Although I didn't study that per se—that's Latin by the way.

(NOTE: Huge round of applause from the Latin Club.)

I did get my education complete, whole, and useful at McGill. I got it in my own way. I urge all of you to get it your way. Don't be afraid of taking chances, of striking out along paths that are untrod. Don't be afraid of failing. Don't be afraid of making an ass of yourself. I do it all the time—and look what I got.

With that, I held my honorary doctorate aloft, as proud as I could possibly be.

I sat back down and scanned the crowd, here at the institution where I started my adult life. In a few weeks, I would also be getting another lifetime achievement honor from the governor general of Canada.

Which reminds me—hey, United States? Let's get busy with the honors and accolades! Do you want to lag behind Canada in the race to honor William Shatner?

So what does one do after so many awards and accolades?

Get to work on winning some more.

There's finality to this life achievement business that I want no part of. As long as you're able to say "yes," the opportunities keep coming, and with them, the adventures. Say "no" to fear and complacency. Keep saying "yes," and the journey will continue.

In this, the eightieth year of my life, I should be settling down, taking it easy, resting on laurels. Forget it.

This rocket ride of a life I'm strapped to just keeps hurtling on and on, faster into the unknown. Will I be ejected, rejected, or dejected? What will happen with my new album? What will happen with this book? With the family? With my TV stuff? The horses? With all the wonderful adventures Elizabeth and I are sharing and will continue to share?

I have no idea. But the rocket keeps going, and I keep holding on.

I think perhaps my rule of saying "yes" has been a way for me to *think* I'm controlling the sometimes wild trajectory of my existence. The fact of the matter is, I've been lucky enough to have life say "yes" to me, time and time again. Perhaps there's no way to control anything. Perhaps the best thing to do is work hard, hold on, and enjoy the view.

I'm not done yet. There are many lives in a lifetime. There are many things I would like to achieve that I haven't. I'll place these degrees, these awards, on my mantel, as a constant reminder of what I have yet to achieve.

Whatever else happens, I'll be sure to let you know. And thanks for saying "yes" to going along on this crazy rocket ride with me.

My best,

Bill

RULE: To Friends, It's Always "Bill"

ACKNOWLEDGMENTS

I would like to thank my editor, Carrie Thornton, who came up with the idea for this book and came calling. I'm glad she did. To her assistant, Stephanie Hitchcock, thank you for being so on top of every detail. Speaking of being on top of every detail, I'd be sunk if it weren't for my assistant, Kathleen Hays, who has all the answers and is always so nice to be around. To our publisher, Brian Tart, our publicist, Amanda Walker, and all of the Dutton/Penguin team I say a hearty *merci*. And to Paul Camuso for keeping me on the cutting edge of that social media thing.

To all my past, present, and future cast mates—I'm sorry for stealing your lunch.

Last but not least, to my fans. Thanks for all the attention. Now give me back my underwear.

6, 146, 174, 227: Courtesy of Paul Camuso

85: Courtesy of *Vegetarian Times*

240: Courtesy of McGill University

FINAL FUN FACTNER:

It's Shatner's World. We Just Live in it.